# FORMULA ONE

# FORMULA ONE

## THE STORY OF GRAND PRIX RACING

NEW
HOLLAND

First published in 2001 by

New Holland (Publishers) Ltd

London • Cape Town • Sydney • Auckland


86 Edgware Road

London W2 2EA

United Kingdom


80 McKenzie Street

Cape Town 8001

South Africa


3/2 Aquatic Drive

Frenchs Forest, NSW 2086

Australia


218 Lake Road

Northcote, Auckland

New Zealand


Consultant Editors: Mark Venables, Behram Kapadia (UK)

Publisher: Mariëlle Renssen

Managing Editors: Claudia Dos Santos (SA),

Mari Roberts (UK)

Managing Art Editor: Peter Bosman

Editors: Romi Bryden, Ingrid Schneider

Design and Illustration: Steven Felmore

Picture researcher: Sonya Meyer

Proofreaders: Chris Whales

Researcher and Indexer: Simon Lewis

Production: Myrna Collins


Reproduction by Hirt & Carter (Cape) Pty Ltd

Printed and bound in Singapore by

Tien Wah Press (Pte) Ltd


10 9 8 7 6 5 4 3 2 1

*Previous pages:* **Ayrton Senna in pole position with Nelson Piquet to the left of him at the start of the 1986 Brazilian Grand Prix in Rio de Janeiro.**

*Left:* **Denny Hulme lifts off at Flugplatz in his McLaren Ford at the Nürburgring during the 1974 German Grand Prix.**

*Following pages:* **The eyes of Benetton driver Alexander Wurz reflect the hunger for success that all Formula One drivers must have to thrive in such a dangerous sport.**

FORMULA ONE

# CONTENTS

# HISTORY

## A BRIEF HISTORICAL OVERVIEW OF GRAND PRIX RACING

The development of the revolutionary internal combustion engine towards the end of the 19th century transformed the world as no other invention has done, before or since. The Germans invented the motor car but the French were fired with the passion to race it, there and then on public roads. Le Vélocipède, the first recorded event on the racing calendar, was won by the only entrant, Count Jules de Dion, on his steam quadricycle. The spectacle stunned the citizens of Paris in 1887 and led to a rash of epic races from this hub: the Paris-Ostend, Paris-Amsterdam-Paris and the Paris-Madrid events. This last, in 1903, caused such carnage that the race was halted in Bordeaux.

Grand Prix events, on circuits closed to other traffic, offered a safe solution that led to the creation of legendary tracks such as Brooklands, in England, and Indianapolis in the USA. In the years prior to World War I, cars underwent dramatic changes as engines shrank from 16 litres to 4.5 litres, while speeds rose proportionately. However, the Great War put an end to racing in Europe. The technological advances that had benefited Grand Prix machines were diverted to powering the engines of war. For the duration, America raced on. European motor racing did not recover from the aftereffects of the conflict until the mid-1920s. By then, Italy, with its Fiats, Bugattis and Alfa Romeos, had overtaken France in the racing stakes.

By the end of the decade, speeds were rising fast, as was the death toll among drivers. Casualties included Antonio Ascari (the father of Alberto Ascari), Jimmy Murphy, Joe Boyer, Dario Resta and Louis Zborowski, the legendary racers of their day. Engine capacities were cut back to 1.5 litres but speeds continued to accelerate rapidly.

When the Depression of the 1930s deprived motorsport of funds, an unexpected windfall arrived in the form of a gift from Germany's Transport Minister, Adolf Hitler. Charged with the task of developing a winning German Grand Prix car, he offered a bonanza of £45,000 to the manufacturer who produced the successful prototype.

Mercedes, Auto-Union and Ferdinand Porsche combined their talents to meet the challenge, sharing the funds. Hitler's endowment led to a revolution in chassis design, in which the use of light alloys and independent suspension on all four wheels played their part. These new models left the rest of the field standing – until the outbreak of World War II called a halt to further innovations.

*Left:* **The first Grand Prix to be staged at Monaco in 1929 was won by William Grover, the only Englishman in the 15-car field, driving a Bugatti 35B. In those days, race organizers gave little thought to the safety of spectators or contestants.**
*Previous pages:* **The safety car follows the grid along the main straight at Interlagos, which has hosted the Brazilian Grand Prix twice since 1990.**

In 1950, the Fédération Internationale de l'Automobile (FIA) decided to create a Formula One world championship for drivers, along the lines of the European championships of 20 years before. The first competition comprised six races in Europe: Great Britain, Monaco, Switzerland, Belgium, France and Italy, as well as the Indianapolis 500 in the USA.

Alfa Romeo, still the favourite, roared into the new formula to claim the inaugural title, with Italy's Giuseppe 'Nino' Farina winning three of the first six races in the new championship. Alfa Romeo repeated this feat in 1951, Juan Manuel Fangio securing the first of his five world championship titles. The subsequent success for Alfa was all the sweeter for the stiff competition coming from the 4.4-litre Ferrari.

Alberto Ascari helped Ferrari to achieve the ascendancy, by winning six of the seven Formula One races in 1952, and five in 1953, to claim both world championship titles. The Italian driver gained the edge while his rival, Fangio, was recovering from injuries sustained in a crash at Monza.

Mercedes entered Formula One again for the 1954 season. They snapped up the best driver on the grid, Fangio, who claimed successive championships for the German marque. Ascari was killed at Monza in 1955, while testing a sports car, just days after surviving a potentially lethal accident in Monaco. Worse followed, when an accident at Le Mans killed 80 spectators. The aftershock caused the cancellation of several world championship events and led to bans in France and Switzerland (a veto that is still in force). The deaths so distressed Lancia that they ceded their racing team to Ferrari and quit the field. Mercedes also stopped racing at the end of the season. British cars had begun to threaten the Italian-German domination of the sport, with the resurgence of BRM and the rise to fame of Connaught in 1955. Fangio moved to Ferrari to take his third consecutive world crown. A fourth followed, this time in a Maserati. The highlight of 1957 was his performance at the Nürburgring, but the Maserati team withdrew at the season's close, as rear-engined cars dominated the field.

From today's perspective, it is shocking how dangerous motor racing was in its infancy. Between 1957 and 1958, no fewer than 12 Formula One drivers lost their lives, a figure that accounted for half the drivers on the grid. Not all of them were killed while competing in Formula One races, however.

**Top left:** German Transport Minister, Adolf Hitler, examines the Mercedes-Benz Rennwagen that he helped finance.
**Top centre:** Henry Birkin and John Cobbs lead at Brookland in 1929.
**Top right:** Giuseppe Campari, of Italy, driving the eight-cylinder Alfa Romeo P2, won the Grand Prix at Lyons in 1924.
*Left:* Fangio finished third in the Lancia-Ferrari D50 at Monaco in 1956.

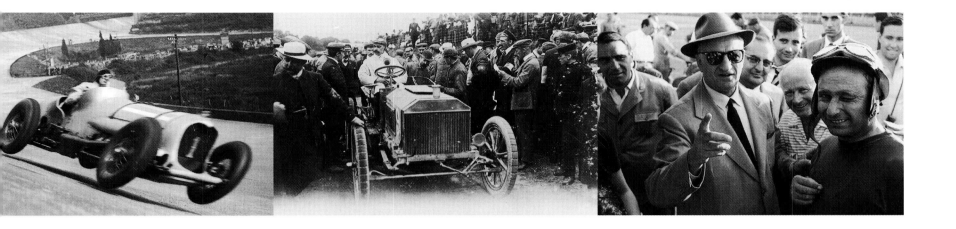

Ken Wharton died in a sports car race in New Zealand; Eugenio Castellotti while testing a Ferrari at Modena; Alfonso de Portago crashed his Ferrari in the Mille Miglia and Piero Carini, another Ferrari driver, also died. Herbert MacKay-Fraser and Bill Whitehouse were killed in a Formula Two race at Reims. Archie Scott-Brown lost his life in a Jaguar at Spa-Francorchamps; Erwin Bauer in a Ferrari at the Nürburgring 1000km; Luigi Musso died during the 1958 French Grand Prix at Reims. Peter Collins died in 1958 at the Nürburgring; Peter Whitehead was killed racing in Australia and Stuart Lewis-Evans died following his crash at the 1958 Moroccan Grand Prix.

Picking his way through the casualties, Mike Hawthorn, in a Ferrari, managed to take the world championship in 1958. Having achieved his goal, he then turned his back on the dangers of motor racing. It is a sad irony that Hawthorn was killed in a motor car accident in January of the following year. Vanwall, the British team, were next to withdraw from motorsport, and the rash of fatalities was believed to be their reason for quitting the field. As drivers died, or left the sport, new names came to the fore. That of Jack Brabham adorned the trophy in 1959; the Australian drove a Cooper Climax. He repeated his triumph the next year by beating his team-mate, Bruce McLaren. Lotus, BRM and even the traditionalists, Ferrari, switched

**Top left: John Cobbs reached an average speed of 230kph (143mph) in the 24-litre, 18-cylinder Napier Railton at Brooklands.**
**Top centre: British company Napier & Sons produced a 45hp car for the Gordon Bennet race in 1903.**
**Top right: Juan Manuel Fangio and Ferrari owner Enzo Ferrari after one of the Argentinian's three victories for the famous Italian team in 1956.**

over to rear-engined cars for 1960, the last year in which victory went to a front-engined racing car. The 1960 Belgian Grand Prix proved to be a grim occasion: two of the drivers, Chris Bristow and Alan Stacey, lost their lives. In addition, two other drivers suffered grave injuries.

The next season, too, was blighted by tragedy. Coming into the final round of the championship at Monza, Wolfgang von Trips was leading Ferrari team-mate Phil Hill by eight points. An accident in the first lap flung Von Trips' Ferrari into the crowd, killing him as well as some 10 spectators. Hill won the race, and eventually the championship, by a point.

Stirling Moss was the next casualty, his Formula One racing career ending after a serious accident before the 1962 championship began.

British teams rose to dominance of the Formula One circuits when they developed the V8 engines, and Graham Hill in the BRM laid claim to the the championship in 1962. Jim Clark followed Hill's lead, winning Lotus' first Drivers' and Constructors' world championship titles in 1963.

The Italians, in the meanwhile, were down but not out: John Surtees raced back with a title for Ferrari in 1964, before Clark earned his second world championship in 1965, again in a Lotus.

The 1966 season began with a splutter as many teams were not able to field one of the latest 3-litre engines. Most of the British teams were caught unprepared, while Ferrari improvised by using their sports car engines. Jack Brabham chose Repco units and claimed the championship in his own car. But there was grim news for his team: the feared Nürburgring claimed yet another life in 1966 when John Taylor died in hospital after a first-lap crash at the German Grand Prix, driving a David Bridges-entered Brabham.

Brabham's fortunes turned, however, when Denny Hulme took a double, winning the 1967 championship ahead of his team leader. Two British

champions, Graham Hill (1968) in a Lotus, and Jackie Stewart (1969) in a Matra, each took the title to bring the swinging Sixties to a close. Sadly, death was never far from the tracks: Jim Clark died in a Formula Two race at Hockenheim in 1968, the same year in which Jo Schlesser was killed in the French Grand Prix, and 1969 brought the death of Gerhard Mitter during practice before the German Grand Prix at the Nürburgring.

The end of this decade, marred by a grisly toll of deaths, was also memorable for one birth – that of commercialism in Formula One, and the arrival of sponsorship. At the Spanish Grand Prix of 1968, the Lotus vehicle sported the red and white of Gold Leaf cigarettes, one bright spot on a small grid. Only 16 cars competed in some events and racing was at a low ebb, a sad reminder of the tally of lives that had been sacrificed to speed.

March, a new entrant to Formula One, swelled the size of the grids in 1970 by making their cars available to customers. The first of these was to be Ken Tyrrell, who had left his partners at Matra.

The list of Formula One fatalities grew. Bruce McLaren died in a Can Am test at Goodwood in the UK, and Piers Courage during the Dutch Grand Prix at Zandvoort. The championship was dominated by Jochen Rindt but, by the end of the season, he too was dead, killed during a practice session at Monza. At the time of his death he was so far ahead of the competition that he was declared world champion, posthumously.

The 1971 season belonged to Jackie Stewart in the Tyrrell. The Scotsman won six of the 11 races on the way to his second world championship. That season ended on a bitter note when Jo Siffert was killed in a non-championship race at Brands Hatch.

By the time the 1972 season got under way, the Brabham team had been sold to Bernie Ecclestone. Switches in sponsorship meant that Lotus had changed into the black and gold of another cigarette brand, John Player Special; McLaren took Yardley's colours, while BRM had a multiple-entry team with the assistance of Marlboro.

After a season-long war of nerves, Emerson Fittipaldi in a Lotus finally triumphed over the champion, Stewart, to take the title. The positions were reversed in 1973, when Stewart beat Fittipaldi. But tragedy struck again, when Roger Williamson was killed driving a March in the Dutch Grand Prix. Then, in the season's final race, François Cevert died driving in the practice laps for the United States Grand Prix at Watkins Glen. In what would have been Stewart's 100th and final race, he walked away from Formula One after the death of his young team-mate.

The number of teams participating in the 1974 Formula One season increased to a record 18 with the addition of the Parnelli and Penske teams. But still the terrible toll of deaths continued to rise; Peter Revson was killed at Kyalami in South Africa and, for the second successive year, a driver was killed at Watkins Glen during the United States Grand Prix. This time it was to be the end of the road for Surtees racer Helmuth Koinigg. Emerson Fittipaldi won that championship by three points from his rival, Clay Regazzoni.

Safety again became an issue. First, the crash-bedevilled Spanish Grand Prix was halted prematurely when an accident occurred involving several spectators. This tragic event was followed by the death of Mark Donohue, killed while practising for the Austrian Grand Prix. However, a new name entered the record that year when Austrian Niki Lauda claimed the trophy.

In the latter part of the 1975 season, the racing world was rocked by the loss of Graham Hill, Tony Brise and four members of their racing team, in an aeroplane crash just north of London.

***Top left:** Graham Hill driving a Gold Leaf Lotus for the Lotus team during the late 1960s, when car designs first began to incorporate wings.*

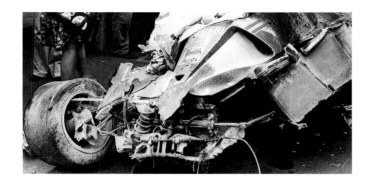

Tom Pryce was killed in 1977 in a bizarre crash involving a marshal, while crossing the line at Kyalami.

For 1976, Fittipaldi moved to his brother's team, which left vacant the plum McLaren seat. This was filled by James Hunt when the Hesketh team withdrew. Then Lauda, the reigning world champion, was lucky to survive a crash at the Nürburgring, but made a swift return to the track in pursuit of his second title. He decided to retire from the final race of the season, in Japan, in dangerously wet weather … and lost his title to Hunt (who finished third in Japan) by a point. He made up for his loss the following season, collecting his second world crown in a year which saw the Ferrari team succumb to sponsorship by wearing Fiat colours.

Arrows, who broke away from the ailing Shadow team, joined the fray in 1978. A brilliant team performance by Lotus' Mario Andretti and Ronnie Peterson (playing second fiddle) ended with the untimely death of Peterson in the Italian Grand Prix at Monza. Unaware that his team-mate was close to death, Andretti managed to secure the championship title with two races in hand.

The decade closed with a world championship win for South African, Jody Scheckter, who gained what was to prove to be Ferrari's last drivers' title for the next 20 years.

By the 1980s, the carnage that had blighted Formula One's first three decades seemed to be a thing of the past. The few tragic accidents that did take place, were all the more poignant for their isolation. A further power struggle between the Fédération Internationale du Sport Automobile (FISA) and the Formula One Constructors' Association (FOCA) heralded the new decade with a dispute that would rumble on for years. And Ron Dennis' Project 4 team merged with McLaren to become McLaren International, the inveterate championship winners.

Alan Jones opened the 1980s by scoring five Grand Prix victories on the way to his only world championship. Driving a Williams, he beat Nelson Piquet, in a Brabham, into second place. Then, in 1981, the Brazilian driver exacted his revenge by taking the title ahead of Williams' new Argentinian driver, Carlos Reutemann.

*Top left:* **The burnt wreck of Niki Lauda's Ferrari at the Nürburgring in 1976. This accident closed the old Nürburgring.**
*Top right:* **Alan Jones won the 1981 USA West Grand Prix at Long Beach.**
*Bottom left:* **Ronnie Peterson at Monaco in the JPS Lotus 78 in May 1978. Four months later he died tragically at Monza.**
*Bottom right:* **Lotus supremo, Colin Chapman, with Ronnie Peterson at the Italian Grand Prix in 1978.**

Williams were back in 1982 in what was to prove a harrowing year for Ferrari. Gilles Villeneuve was killed in the Belgian Grand Prix at Zolder. At Hockenheim his team-mate, Didier Pironi, who had taken the lead, suffered terrible injuries to his legs in an accident. Pironi and Riccardo Paletti (Osella) collided in practice at Canada – Paletti died in hospital. With four races remaining Keke Rosberg in the Williams was 16 points adrift of the Italian. However, a hat-trick of truly excellent finishes landed him the title.

Colin Chapman, the genius behind Lotus, died suddenly at the end of the 1982 season. His passing led to Lotus' gradual decline.

Brazil's Nelson Piquet took the crown for Brabham by two points in 1983, driving the first turbo-charged car. He snatched this victory from budding talent Alain Prost, achieving a third place finish in the final race of the season, the South African Grand Prix at Kyalami.

The TAG Porsche-powered McLaren was the dominant car for 1984 and the title ended in a straight fight between the two McLaren men, Lauda and Prost. Lauda lifted the trophy with half a point to spare after a titanic battle, trailing Prost to the chequered flag at Estoril in the season finale.

McLaren merged with TAG for 1985, and Prost cruised to his first world championship in the powerful machine.

**Top left: Alain Prost on the podium at Monaco with Prince Rainier. The Frenchman won four times in the principality.**
**Top right: Ayrton Senna, who won at Monaco six times, on the way to his third victory in 1990.**
**Left: Trevor Taylor leads the field through Radillon at the 1960 Belgium Grand Prix as the back of the pack thread their way through Eau Rouge, the most famous corner in Formula One.**

The Williams FW11 was car of the year for 1986 with Nigel Mansell and Piquet the fortunate drivers, but the team suffered a dire setback when Frank Williams was paralysed in a road traffic accident. The season-long battle between the Williams drivers was concluded by a victory at Adelaide for McLaren's Alain Prost who took the championship. Mansell's notorious exploding tyre dashed the Englishman's hopes of a win – and the championship – with 19 laps left to run in the race and, indeed, in the season.

The Williams pair clashed again the following year, but Piquet had the upper hand for most of 1987 and clinched the title when Mansell injured his neck at Suzuka towards the close of the season.

Another great team leader left the circuit in 1988 – Ferrari's founder, Enzo Ferrari, died in August at the age of 90. It was a year monopolized by Ayrton Senna and Alain Prost in the McLarens, their cars powered by the awesome Honda V6 turbos, when Senna snatched eight wins to Prost's seven. It seemed appropriate that the only contest they didn't win was the big race following Enzo Ferrari's death. This, the Italian Grand Prix at Monza, was won on an emotional occasion by Gerhard Berger in a Ferrari.

The celebrated duel between Prost and Senna continued in 1989 but grew more acrimonious as the season progressed. It was finally decided when Prost drove the Brazilian off the track at the Suzuka chicane. Although Senna managed to start again and win that race, he was later disqualified for getting push started, and the championship went to Prost.

The French driver transferred to Ferrari for the 1990 campaign, but the battle raged on. Smarting from Prost's tactic a year earlier, Senna took his rival out at the first corner, claiming both retribution and the championship title.

A new entrant for 1991 was Eddie Jordan and his Jordan Grand Prix team, who had an impressive début season in their 7-Up-liveried Jordan-Ford 191, although Bertrand Gachot found himself in a British jail after an incident in traffic. For the Belgian Grand Prix, his place was taken by the young Michael Schumacher. Senna finished the year as champion again. This time his closest challenger was Mansell, who had never won a title, in the Williams. Finally, 1992 was to prove Mansell's great year. His mount, the Williams FW14B, was almost unbeatable and he won eight of the first 10 races to secure the crown with five races yet to run. Despite this success he and Williams parted company and he was replaced by Prost.

In 1993 Prost secured his fourth world championship, but he opted for retirement with the news that Senna was to join Williams in 1994. Senna tried his hand but luck was not on his side. The gifted Brazilian crashed and died at Imola in a weekend that also claimed the life of Roland Ratzenberger. The first Grand Prix fatalities in 12 years came as a shock as many believed modern Formula One cars (and their drivers) to be invincible.

Schumacher, aboard the Benetton, was the man to beat in 1994 and – after winning six of the first seven races – he was a massive 37 points clear of Damon Hill, who had moved up to lead the Williams team after Senna's death. Hill closed the gap and at Adelaide, in the final race of the season, he was only one point behind. Hill trailed Schumacher, who in a move reminiscent of Prost's baulking of Senna at Suzuka in 1989, took Hill out of the race. Schumacher claimed his first world championship in a thoroughly unsatisfactory manner. He repeated the feat, more sportingly, the next year when Hill was again his main challenger.

It all fell into place for Hill in 1996, however, when he at long last took the crown. Frank Williams rewarded him by dropping him for 1997.

Williams again controlled the contest that year and Hill's former teammate, Jacques Villeneuve, stepped up to take the world title. It was an accolade that had eluded his late father, Gilles, in his six-season career.

After a spell in the wilderness, McLaren came roaring back to life when their alliance with Mercedes powered them back into the front row of the grid. The man to benefit from this combination was Mika Hakkinen. The Finn had the honour of celebrating the 50th anniversary of Formula One by winning the 1998 and 1999 world championships in fine style. Ferrari's Michael Schumacher ended Hakkinen's dominance in 2000, winning the last four races of the season to claim his third title.

**Right: Alain Prost (left) and Ayrton Senna spent two tempestuous years together at McLaren – it ended in acrimony at the Suzuka chicane in 1989, when Prost won the championship by driving into his team-mate.**

CIGARETTES
Marlbor
GOODYEAR
elf
Tyrrell
4
DEPAILLER
p. depailler
elf
GOODYEAR
elf
GOODYEAR
4
elf

# TECHNOLOGY

## REGULATIONS AND DEVELOPMENTS

Any competition or championship must be governed by a comprehensive set of rules and, when that sport includes not just the human element, the driver, but an ever-evolving mechanical aspect, the car, then the regulations are bound to be subject to change. This is the case with Formula One motorsport. In its early days racing was relatively open but as big business and the high-tech industry have hijacked the sport, the rule makers have taken on an ever more important role.

This brief guide to rule changes over the first 50 years of Formula One must treat each topic fleetingly, and some not at all. The sporting and technical regulations of the Fédération Internationale de l'Automobile (FIA) which cover Formula One, are revised annually and run to hundreds of pages each year, which explains why they are condensed here.

When the Formula One championship was created in 1950, in the post-war depression, the rules were formulated to suit the machinery that was then available. Cars could be either supercharged or non-supercharged, with capacity limits of 1.5 litres and 4.5 litres respectively.

*Left: The six-wheel Tyrrell, designed by Derek Gardner, had quite a successful debut session in 1976. The highlight was the one-two that Jody Scheckter and Patrick Depailler achieved in the Swedish Grand Prix in June.*

Each driver's best results counted towards the championship and this system was maintained until the 1991 season, with the number of races which counted fluctuating between four and 11, depending on how many races made up the championship. Points were awarded from first down to fifth places (8, 6, 4, 3, 2), together with a point for the fastest lap. With entrants relatively scarce, the rules were changed after two seasons and, for the 1952 campaign, the current Formula Two category rules were adopted: 2-litre non-supercharged and 500cc supercharged, with no weight limits.

By 1954 it was deemed appropriate to return to Formula One specifications and the 2.5-litre formula was introduced with supercharged engines of 750cc also allowed.

Racing was a gentlemanly pursuit in its early days – there was not the rush of innovations and new cars. The first major new development arrived in 1956, when disc brakes made their appearance. This was followed by the introduction of the rear-engined Coopers SZ.

New fuel regulations were announced for 1958, compelling cars to run on commercial petrol, which meant that aviation fuel to 130 octane was adopted. The length of races was reduced to a maximum of 300km (186,42 miles) or two hours and no points were to be awarded for shared drives. This was also the first year in which the Constructors' Championship was awarded to the team having won the most points.

For the first campaign of the Sixties, the point for fastest lap was dropped and replaced by a point for sixth place. Lotus, BRM and even the traditionalist Ferrari turned to rear-engined cars; 1960 was the last year for a victory by a front-engined car.

A minimum weight of the car containing water and oil, but excluding a fuel allowance of 450kg (992.3lb), was introduced for 1961 with engines limited to 1.5-litre maximum and 1.3-litre minimum. The points awarded for a race win were also increased to nine.

Ever the innovators, Lotus re-introduced the monocoque (a car in which the chassis and the body are a unit) to top line racing with the Type 25 model for 1962, a move that was soon copied by all the major teams.

Further restrictions on the awarding of points were introduced in 1963. Drivers had to complete two-thirds of the race distance to be classified and qualify for points.

Attention turned to the benefits to be gained from tyres, which resulted in the development of wider treads for the 1965 season.

The seemingly endless alteration of engine specifications continued in the 1966 season with engine capacity being enlarged to 3 litres or 1.5 litres for supercharged engines. The minimum weight was also increased to 500kg (1102.5lb) while the distance a driver was required to complete before being classified, was increased to 90 per cent of the race distance.

The late-Sixties saw the first signs of Formula One's emergence as the sport we know today. The season of 1967, in particular, was a landmark for Formula One racing. At the Dutch Grand Prix at Zandvoort the Ford Cosworth DFV V8 made its first appearance, powering Jim Clark's Lotus 40 to victory. That engine, or its derivatives, would go on to win 10 world championships and open up Formula One to customer engine packages. Manually operated wings came into play at the Belgian Grand Prix of 1968,

giving drivers their first experience of aerodynamic aids. Innovations were continually being introduced, ever in pursuit of even the slightest advantage. Lotus, McLaren and Matra all tried out four-wheel drive technology during the 1969 season but it was promptly banned.

Lotus went for something new again in 1970, showing their wedge-shaped Lotus 72, the shape created by placing the radiators on either side of the cockpit.

Slick tyres made their first appearance in 1971, along with substantially wider tyres. Air scoops above the driver's head, that forced air into the engine under pressure, were introduced by Lotus on its turbo car at selected races.

With the increasing speed and complexity of Formula One machines, safety became a major issue of concern; deformable structures were required for the Spanish race, and after the Dutch race, all grids became two-by-two formations. The minimum weight was increased again, this time to 575kg (1267.9lb).

Ferrari introduced the 312T transverse gearbox for the 1975 season and the following year Tyrrell briefly unveiled its unique six-wheeled car.

Lotus made another significant step forward in car design in 1977, with the Lotus 78 wing car, a car with wings to generate grip through aerodynamic downforce. Renault also introduced the first turbo to world championship racing, designed to comply with the equivalent formula of 1.5 litres.

*Top left:* **In 1950 and 1951, Fangio won six races for the Alfa Corse team.**
*Top centre:* **Jim Clark raced for Lotus for nine years, winning 25 races for the trend-setting British team.**
*Top right:* **Colin Chapman introduced various innovations to Formula One, including aerodynamic aids, four-wheel drive and the wedge shape.**

The Lotus cars which followed further developed the Lotus 78 model, with skirts along the sidepods to prevent air from escaping. In an attempt to take this tactic a step further, Brabham created the fan car; however, after a maiden victory, it was banned.

As the decade closed, the rapidly changing power base of engines was emphasized when a turbo engine won for the first time. Not only were engines evolving but the materials used in the manufacture of race cars was changing. Carbon fibre is de rigueur in modern Formula One but it made its first appearance as far back as 1979, when it featured in the Brabham chassis.

The document that controlled the rules and the structure of Formula One was created in 1981. Called the Concorde Agreement, it came about as a result of a dispute Fédération Internationale du Sport Automobile (FISA) and the Formula One Constructors' Association (FOCA).

A ban on ground effects skirts as well as a 6mm (0.25in) ground clearance was also agreed upon although the latter was soon overcome with the aid of various hydraulic devices. In a further development of Brabham's efforts both McLaren and Lotus built entire carbon-fibre chassis, rendering aluminium monocoques obsolete.

With rigid suspension and the grip created by aerodynamic devices, cornering speeds and the G-forces to which drivers were subjected were

increasing year by year. This resulted in new regulations being introduced for 1983. The ban on skirts prevailed and it was decided that all cars should have flat bottoms.

In the fast-moving world of Formula One no sooner has one danger been removed than the teams, in their quest for those vital seconds, come up with another ruse to increase performance. This time it was the Brabham team who, after experiments during 1982, adopted a strategy for the 1983 season that demanded refuelling.

Safety issues forced a refuelling ban a year later and teams were limited to 220 litres (48.4 gall) of fuel per car. Turbos were dominant, and only Tyrrell used a normally aspirated engine. However, they were banned for weight deception after ball-bearings were found in tanks at post-race scrutineering.

For 1986 only 1.5-litre turbos were permitted, with a new fuel allowance of 195 litres (43 gall). These were limited to a maximum boost of 4.0 bar the following year, by means of a compulsory pop-off valve - and that was further reduced to 2.5 bar for the 1988 season. Fuel was also restricted to 150 litres (33 gall) for 1988, making some races more a matter of fuel economy than outright speed.

Lotus had showcased its Active Suspension system in 1987, which utilized computer-controlled hydraulics to optimize the ride height of the car at any given position on the track.

Turbo engines were finally banned in 1989 with only 3.5-litre atmospheric engines permitted. The minimum weight was reduced to 500kg (1102.5 lb). There were no restrictions on the amount of fuel but refuelling was still not allowed

On the technical front Ferrari, who had been in the doldrums, produced the revolutionary semi-automatic gearbox in which gear changes were controlled by switches on the steering wheel.

*Top left:* **Mario Andretti in the John Player Special Lotus. The English team pioneered sponsorship in the 1970s.**
*Top centre:* **An early version of wings on the Brabham BT20 at Monaco, 1967.**
*Top right:* **Heinz-Harald Frentzen and Patrick Head, the Williams technical director, examine the front brakes.**

# Tyres

On a race weekend, the driver must not use more than 32 dry-weather tyres and 28 wet-weather tyres. Before qualifying, the driver must choose between the two specifications of dry-weather tyre available. The choice he makes then must be retained for the rest of the race weekend.

The tyres currently in use all have grooves. This is because of FIA regulations aimed at reducing the grip supplied, thereby reducing cornering speeds, which in the wake of Ayrton Senna's fatal accident they deemed to be dangerously high. In the past, qualifying tyres consisting of special high grip rubber that lasted for only one or two laps, were employed by most teams. They have since been banned due to the escalating cost.

# GREAT DRIVERS

## HEROES WHO DOMINATED THE GRAND PRIX RACING STAGE

## JUAN MANUEL FANGIO

Born: 24 June 1911 • Died: 17 July 1995

No man has dominated Formula One as completely as the amazing Argentinian, Juan Manuel Fangio. In the seven full seasons during which he raced (beginning with the inaugural world championship in 1950), Fangio won the championship five times and finished second in his two other seasons. In his short career he entered 51 Grands Prix, winning nearly half of them, and achieved a win-to-start ratio that has never been bettered.

The son of Italian immigrants, Fangio was born in Balcarce, Argentina, in 1911. After completing his national service he opened a garage and began driving in local races. In Argentina, the 'local races' differed from club meetings in Europe: they were long distance races

*Left:* **Stirling Moss (left) congratulates Juan Manuel Fangio following the Argentinian's victory at the British Grand Prix at Silverstone in 1956.** *Previous pages:* **Fangio driving the Mercedes-Benz W196 at the Spanish Grand Prix in 1954.**

run up and down the length of the South American continent. Fangio's first victory came at the age of 18, when he drove a taxi to success in the Gran Premio del Norte, a 16,000km (10,000-mile) marathon through the Andes and back to Argentina, that took two weeks to run.

Just after World War II, Fangio was sponsored by the Argentine government to race in Europe. For his first season in Formula One, Fangio drove the all-conquering Alfa Romeo alongside Giuseppe 'Nino' Farina. Between them, they won all six of the Formula One Grands Prix, three each, but Farina just pipped Fangio to the crown. The only race to slip through their grasp was the 805km (500-mile) Indy 500 that formed part of the championship in its early days.

Fangio won a further three races in 1951, enabling him to claim his first championship ahead of the Ferrari of Alberto Ascari. The following year was bleak for Fangio, who broke his neck at Monza after his car hit an earth bank and somersaulted. He hovered close to death for several hours, survived the accident, but missed the entire season.

He was back for 1953, this time driving a Maserati, but he could muster just one victory at Monza and had to console himself with a second place in the championship.

The next four seasons were a different matter. Such was Fangio's domination of Formula One that he won an astonishing 17 of the races run (driving in three different cars). Fangio won the two opening races of the 1954 season in a Maserati, then switched to Mercedes, reeling

off four more race victories to claim his second championship. The following season he was in the Mercedes and picked up four great wins to claim his third championship. The Argentinian made it all look so effortless and went on to collect his fourth world championship title in 1956, this time for Ferrari, when three race wins were sufficient to clinch the title. Fangio returned to Maserati in 1957 and won a further four races to give him the world championship for the fifth time. His first place at the Nürburgring that season was the scene of his last great triumph.

At the age of 46 Fangio started the following season with Maserati, but he only contested two races before deciding that he had lost his edge. Fangio's final act of courage was to walk away from the sport of which he had for so long been the dominant force.

*Above:* **Fangio driving the Lancia-Ferrari D50 at Monaco in 1956. The Argentinian was the first of the great post-War drivers, winning five world titles, his last in 1957 at the age of 46.**
*Below:* **Fangio reunited with one of his title-winning Alfa Romeo 159 *Alfetta* cars in an historic round-the-houses run at Montreux, Switzerland.**
*Right:* **The Mercedes-Benz W194 that Fangio drove to his second title in 1954 is put through its paces at Aintree in the 1955 British Grand Prix.**

## ACHIEVEMENTS

| | |
|---|---|
| Grands Prix contested | 51 |
| Grand Prix victories | 24 |
| Pole positions | 28 |
| Podium finishes | 35 |
| World championships | 1951, 1954, 1955, 1956, 1957 |

claim the maximum points (only the four best results were counted), with victories at Spa-Francorchamps, Rouen, Silverstone, the Nürburgring, Zandvoort and Monza.

In 1953 he won the championship again, this time with five victories – the challenge from Fangio and Farina having become very much tougher. Two Maserati outings and solo drives for Ferrari and Lancia took Ascari through 1954 before he switched to the brand-new Lancia team for the fateful season of 1955.

Driving in the Monaco Grand Prix of 1955 in pursuit of Lancia's first Grand Prix victory, the Italian was gaining a couple of seconds per lap on the dominant Mercedes, calling upon every ounce of his skill. Ascari was in second place, chasing Stirling Moss in his Mercedes Silver Arrow. At the start of the 81st lap Ascari was still charging, while unbeknown to the Italian driver (this was before the advent of pit-to-car radio), Moss had been forced to retire.

# ALBERTO ASCARI

Born: 13 July 1918 • Died: 26 May 1955

Alberto was born in 1918 in Milan, to the family of Antonio Ascari, a great Italian driver of his day. Just before Alberto turned seven, Antonio was killed in a race in France. From that moment on, Alberto was committed to emulating his famous father's racing achievements.

He began his quest to be the world champion driver in the renowned Mille Miglia, behind the wheel of a Ferrari. Before he took part in the inaugural world championship season of 1950, Alberto had married a girl from his hometown and had two children, Antonio (who was named after his late grandfather) and Patrizia.

Alberto raced for Ferrari in four of the seven races held in 1950, but the best he could manage were a pair of second place finishes, at Monaco and Monza. The next year he collected his maiden world championship victory at the Nürburgring, following that up with a win at Monza, on the way to second place in the championship. In 1952 he won the world crown at a canter, becoming Ferrari's first world champion. Ascari was able to

*Above:* **Alberto Ascari in a Ferrari during the 1953 French Grand Prix in which he finished fourth.**

*Top left:* **Alberto Ascari celebrates victory in the 1953 British Grand Prix.**

Now in the lead, Ascari might have been distracted by the flag-waving crowd, and he made a grave miscalculation approaching the chicane that skirts the harbour, just after the tunnel. He lost control of the car and ploughed through the protective hay bales, across the quay and into the harbour. He was quickly fished out of the water and was fortunate to have sustained no more than shock and a badly broken nose.

Four days later, while he was watching the preliminary practice runs for a sports car race at Monza, Alberto decided that he would like to do a couple of laps in a friend's Ferrari. Wearing his street clothes and a borrowed helmet he set off, full of confidence. While he was on his third lap, the car inexplicably went into a skid and somersaulted, throwing him out onto the track. Ascari suffered multiple injuries and died at the scene of the accident. He was only 37 years old.

Three days after his funeral, Lancia decided to suspend all their racing operations. Later that year they handed their cars, engines and blueprints for future vehicles over to Ferrari.

To the stricken Italians, Alberto Ascari's death at Monza, so close to the city of his birth, was a national tragedy. The main square, the Piazza del Duomo, in Milan was packed to capacity for his funeral and the normally noisy and bustling city centre was brought to a silent standstill. A much-loved champion, Ascari's memory lives on in the hearts of his countrymen and in those of his many fans all over the world.

## A C H I E V E M E N T S

| | |
|---|---|
| Grands Prix contested | 32 |
| Grand Prix victories | 13 |
| Pole positions | 14 |
| Podium finishes | 19 |
| World championships | 1952, 1953 |

*Top right:* **Jack Brabham won the world championship three times – in 1959 and in 1960 – driving a Cooper Climax. Six years later he was victorious again, this time aboard the Brabham BT19, making him the only Formula One driver to win the championship in his own car.**

# JACK BRABHAM

Born: 2 April 1926

Jack Brabham will be best remembered for establishing the Brabham team that competed in 394 Grands Prix, gaining 35 victories and two Constructors' Championships. Jack, himself, however, enjoyed his greatest success driving cars for Cooper.

Brabham was a second generation Australian; his father was a Sydney grocer who had taught young Jack to drive at an early age. Brabham later developed a passion for cars that led him to leave school at 15 to work in a garage during the day while studying engineering at night school.

After a stint in the Australian Air Force, Brabham set up a garage of his own and began to race Midget cars, along with Johnny Schonberg.

Oporto, to claim back-to-back championships. As the Cooper star waned, Brabham started to put his plan into action. He set up a team of his own, with the help of Ron Tauranac. The Brabham team made its debut at the Nürburgring in 1962. Dan Gurney could claim only two victories for them in 1964, as they struggled with the new 1.5-litre formula. It was not until 1966, when the 3-litre formula came into play, that Brabham really came into their own.

Armed with the Australian Repco engine, Brabham was back on the winning trail and tied up his third and final world championship with victories at Reims, the Nürburgring, Brands Hatch and Zandvoort. Jack's hunger for a fourth world title was undiminished. He collected his 12th and 13th Grand Prix victories in 1967, at Le Mans and Mosport respectively, but still just fell short of the title. There was, however, some small consolation in the fact that Denny Hulme of New Zealand could claim the title in the second Brabham.

When Schonberg decided to quit the racing scene, Brabham continued, going on to win the New South Wales championship. He also forged a friendship with Ron Tauranac that was to stand him in good stead in the future.

Jack made his Formula One debut in 1955, driving the Cooper at Aintree. The following year he competed at Silverstone in a Maserati. Brabham spent the next two years driving a Cooper Climax without any noteworthy results.

It was not until 1959, when the Cooper featured the Coventry Climax 2.5-litre engine, that success came his way. His victories at Monaco and Aintree were sufficient to earn him the world championship ahead of the British pair of Tony Brooks, in the Ferrari, and Stirling Moss, in the BRM.

In 1960, driving the new lowline Cooper, Brabham reeled off a string of five victories at Zandvoort, Spa-Francorchamps, Reims, Silverstone and

The Brabham team could find no response to the pace of the Lotus Ford in 1968. Having secured the impressive Ford Cosworth for 1969, Jack's campaign was thwarted by a broken ankle. That, he decided, would be a very good time to call it a day. The conspicuous absence of a top-flight driver who could take his place in the Brabham team was the only factor that persuaded him to continue for one more season. He was rewarded with a win at the season-opener at Kyalami, his final Formula One victory, although he came close at Monaco where he was leading until he was passed by Jochen Rindt at the last corner. He retired after the Mexican Grand Prix of that year.

*Above:* **Jack Brabham won 14 Grands Prix over his 16-year Formula One career, his final triumph coming at Kyalami in South Africa in 1970, where he drove the Brabham BT33 to victory.**

# A C H I E V E M E N T S

| | |
|---|---|
| Grands Prix contested | 126 |
| Grand Prix victories | 14 |
| Pole positions | 13 |
| Podium finishes | 31 |
| World championships | 1959, 1960, 1966 |

# GRAHAM HILL

Born: 17 February 1929 • Died: 29 November 1975

*Left:* **Graham Hill retired from Formula One to run his own team, after suffering terrible injuries at Watkins Glen. However, his new career was cut short when he was killed in a plane crash in 1975.**

Graham Hill was a very successful driver who came into the sport relatively late in life. Although he raced for 18 years and was a double world champion, Hill averaged less than a win a year, securing just 14 Grand Prix victories in total.

Born in London, Hill's desire for a career behind the wheel of a race car was sparked by an advertisement for a racing school. The lure of laps at

*Below:* **Graham Hill returned to Lotus for fours years, from 1967 to 1971, winning three races and the world championship in 1968 for the England-based team.**

the Brands Hatch Formula One circuit – for five shillings a time – was too strong to shun. Hill offered his experience as a mechanic in exchange for laps and, although the promised laps never materialized, his ambition to race had been fired.

After further forays into racing schools, Hill met Colin Chapman who employed him as a mechanic at the Lotus plant. However, he wanted to race for Chapman, not work on cars. In a scenario that seems improbable today, Hill managed to convince Chapman to take a chance on him and he made his Formula One debut in the Lotus Climax at Monaco in 1958. He retained his seat at Lotus for two seasons without managing to finish in the top six, before joining up with BRM for 1960.

Success was hard to come by and it was the opening round of his third season with BRM before he scored his first win at the Dutch Grand Prix at Zandvoort. His appetite whetted, Hill gained two further victories in August that year, at the Nürburgring and Monza, before winning the last race of the season, held in East London, South Africa. His triumphs won him the world championship by eight points from Jim Clark in the Lotus.

He spent four more years at BRM, collecting a further six titles, three each at Monaco and the USA. His car was dogged by mechanical failures and he was unable to repeat his success, so he returned to Lotus in 1967, nine years after Chapman had given him his start in Formula One racing. Rejoining Lotus, Hill teamed up with Jim Clark, a partnership that was destined to be cut short by Clark's untimely death at Hockenheim in 1968.

Hill went on to win the two races after Hockenheim and became world champion for the second time. The following year was not successful, the one bright spot being his fifth win on the tricky Monaco circuit. This was to be his final Formula One victory.

Hill's incredible record of five wins in the principality was to remain intact until 1993, when Brazilian driver, Ayrton Senna, surpassed his impressive tally by claiming a sixth victory.

Although Hill raced on for a further six years, at Lotus, Brabham, Shadow and Lola, he did not visit the podium again. Injuries he sustained at Watkins Glen, though not fatal, were severe enough to confine him to a wheelchair for some time. Unable to recapture the winning form of his earlier days, in 1975 he decided to stop racing and form his own team.

The world of racing lost yet another of its favourite sons in November, 1975, when Hill was killed in an aviation accident.

## A C H I E V E M E N T S

| | |
|---|---|
| Grands Prix contested | 176 |
| Grand Prix victories | 14 |
| Pole positions | 13 |
| Podium finishes | 36 |
| World championships | 1962, 1968 |

# STIRLING MOSS

Born: 17 September 1929

Stirling Moss was the epitome of the English gentleman racing driver who graced the racetracks of the world from the late-1940s through to the early-1960s. His unfortunate fate – to be remembered as the best driver never to win a world championship. With a record 16 victories from 66 races there cannot be another Formula One driver more deserving of the ultimate accolade. As it turned out, he had to settle for four runner-up and three third-place championships.

Unlike most Formula One racers, Moss seemed destined to race. He was born into a racing family: his father competed at Brooklands, his mother in rallies and trials. His father bought him his first car, an Austin Seven, in which he learned his trade in the fields that surrounded their country home. Although racing was in his blood, Moss first toyed with other careers. When poor grades prevented him from becoming a dentist like his father, he tried his hand at the hotel trade, where he worked as both a waiter and night porter.

The lure of the motor car was too powerful, however, and when Moss saw a newspaper advertisement for an Aspen-powered racing car for £50, he ordered one. His father cancelled the order but he allowed Stirling to drive his BMW in local time trials.

Moss' career was patchy – he drove his way through hillclimbs to Formula Two with the HWM team and then on to Jaguar C-type.

It appeared that Moss would be offered a chance to drive a spare Ferrari in 1951, but at the first race of the season he was told that Piero Taruffi would drive it – a snub that Moss was never to forget.

His first race was the Swiss Grand Prix at Bremgarten in a British HWM. The following year he raced once more for HWM, as well as for two other UK teams – three races for ERA and a single outing in the Connaught, at Monza, without success. In fact, in the early years of Italian and German dominance, Moss paid a heavy price for his loyalty to British machines. Following another winless season with Connaught and Cooper, Moss made a move to the Italian Maserati team for the 1954 campaign, teaming up for a single race with Fangio. The Argentinian went across to Mercedes – a move that Moss would duplicate the following year.

The 1955 season marked his first Formula One win, at Aintree, in the British Grand Prix. When Mercedes quit Formula One at the end of that year Moss returned to Maserati, while Fangio went to Lancia. Although Moss claimed two victories, at Monaco and Monza, by the end of the year Fangio was ahead by three points.

The pair were back together again with Maserati for 1957, but again their liaison was brief, with Moss moving to Vanwall after the season-opening Argentine Grand Prix. Once again they dominated the championship. Moss claimed three victories, but for the third successive year he trailed Fangio, this time by 15 points. When Fangio retired midway

through the 1958 season, he left the field clear for Moss to claim the elusive championship, but it was not to be. Despite winning four races to Mike Hawthorn's one, he lost the title by one point to his countryman.

Despite two wins each year for the following three years, Moss was never again to get so close to winning the title. His career was brought to an end following a high-speed accident at Goodwood in 1962 when he was fortunate to escape with his life. After making a slow recovery he decided against a return to Formula One. Reluctant to leave the track altogether, Stirling Moss went on to race touring cars and still races in historic events.

*Above:* **A pensive Stirling Moss at Monza in 1954.**

*Inset:* **Stirling Moss, retired from Formula One since 1961, is still a popular personality with a host of public engagements.**

*Left:* **Moss driving his Maserati 250F in pursuit of Fangio's Mercedes Benz W196, at the Spanish Grand Prix in Pedralbes in 1954.**

## A C H I E V E M E N T S

| | |
|---|---|
| Grands Prix contested | 66 |
| Grand Prix victories | 16 |
| Pole positions | 16 |
| Podium finishes | 24 |
| World championships | None |

# JIM CLARK

Born: 4 March 1936 • Died: 7 April 1968

Clark features high on the all-time-greats lists of motorsport writers. This enigmatic Scotsman, who hailed from a small Scottish farming community in Fife, competed in 72 Grands Prix before his untimely death. In the course of the nine seasons in which he raced, he collected two world championships, and amassed 25 victories and 33 pole positions.

Clark's family did not want him to race and his early career was limited to rallies and local races. He stepped up to sports cars for the Border Reivers, run by Jock McBain and, ironically, he even raced against a Lotus driven by a certain Colin Chapman.

His Formula One break came when his skill behind the wheel of a private Aston Martin impressed Reg Parnell, the factory team manager. Aston Martin were planning to enter Formula One and assigned Clark as test driver, a role he intended to share with his contract for Colin Chapman's Formula Two outfit. The Aston Martin Formula One car was to be a non-runner, and their entry was cancelled. In the meantime, such was the impression he had made on Colin Chapman that he was offered a Formula One drive by Lotus.

In 1960 he made his lacklustre debut at Zandvoort before moving on to the awe-inspiring Spa-Francorchamps, which still retained its daunting 14.5km (9 mile) layout. In spite of the fearsome reputation of Spa (it had claimed two lives that year including that of Clark's team-mate, Alan Stacey), he won a brave and creditable fifth place.

The following year Clark raced eight times with little success. He was, however, involved in a controversial incident during the penultimate race of the season, at Monza. Clark's Lotus came into contact with the Ferrari of Wolfgang von Trips, sending his car flying into the crowd. Von Trips died in the accident, and some 10 unsuspecting spectators also lost their lives.

Clark began the 1962 season full of hope but mechanical failures deprived him of points in the first two races at Zandvoort and Monaco. A mid-season run of three victories was initiated by his maiden Formula One triumph at Spa-Francorchamps, a race that he would go on to win in four consecutive seasons. His charge towards the championship was halted

in the final race of the season; unfortunately for Clark, he had once again been thwarted by mechanical gremlins.

After the disappointment of losing out on the championship in 1962, Clark dominated in 1963 with seven wins from the 10 championship races. He sprinted to the title well ahead of second-placed Graham Hill.

The following season was a much tighter affair, with Clark facing a season-long battle with Graham Hill and John Surtees in a Ferrari. With three victories to add to his growing tally, Clark arrived at the season's finale in Mexico needing a win to be sure of the title ahead of his two rivals. Hill dropped out early on and Clark appeared to be heading for back-to-back crowns, until an engine seizure handed the title to Surtees.

In 1965 it was more of the same, with another Scot, Jackie Stewart, also in contention. Clark triumphed with six more victories. The introduction of the 3-litre category in 1966 saw Lotus struggling and, although he claimed his 20th Grand Prix victory at Watkins Glen, it was a disheartening campaign.

The arrival of the Ford-Cosworth DFV, for the third race of 1967, restored the team's competitive edge. However, that victory, followed by three others at Silverstone, Watkins Glen and Mexico, were good for no more than a third place in the championship.

Jim Clark started the 1968 season full of promise with a victory at Kyalami, but it was to be his final Grand Prix appearance. Tragically, at the age of 32, he died in a Formula Two race at Hockenheim in Germany before the second Grand Prix of the season.

## ACHIEVEMENTS

| | |
|---|---|
| Grands Prix contested | 72 |
| Grand Prix victories | 25 |
| Pole positions | 33 |
| Podium finishes | 32 |
| World championships | 1963, 1965 |

*Right:* **Jim Clark ready for the start of the 1964 British Grand Prix at Brands Hatch. The Scotsman started from pole position and recorded his third victory from the first five races of the season.**

*Inset:* **Jim Clark shows the strain of an unsuccessful 1964 campaign.**

# JACKIE STEWART

Born: 11 June 1939

*Left:* Jackie Stewart retired from Formula One in 1973, having just won his third Drivers' Championship.

John Young Stewart was born in Milton, Dunbartonshire, Scotland, just before World War II. The love of cars ran in Stewart's family. His elder brother, Jimmy, was the first of the family to take to racing, but an accident put a premature end to his hopes of a career in motorsport.

Against the wishes of his mother, Jackie followed his brother into the field, opening what was to be his illustrious career with a race in a Porsche at Oulton Park in 1962. Two years later, one of the sport's most successful pairings began when Stewart teamed up with Ken Tyrrell to race the latter's Coopers in Formula Three. Stewart was on the pace right from the start, winning his first Formula Three race at Snetterton in Norfolk. Stewart soon moved up to Formula Two with Tyrrell, before being lured by BRM in 1965, for his first taste of Formula One. He was to partner the successful Graham Hill. On his Formula One debut, Stewart finished sixth in the South African Grand Prix at East London, where he scored just a single point. He went on to win his first race at Monza, later that year. It soon became apparent that a new star had been born.

Jackie Stewart won the opening round of the 1966 campaign at Monaco, but at Spa, a sudden downpour rendered the circuit extremely hazardous and several cars left the track. Jackie's was one of them. He landed in a ditch, drenched with petrol and unable to free himself, because his legs were trapped by the steering wheel.

With the help of a toolkit borrowed from a nearby spectator, it took his fellow-drivers, Bob Bondurant and Graham Hill, more than 30 minutes to get Stewart out. The injured driver was then left lying on a stretcher in the rain before, finally, he was taken to hospital.

From that day on, Stewart campaigned to make motor racing safer, a crusade he was to carry on long after he had retired from the track. He started his lobby with the assistance of the head of the BRM team, Louis Stanley, beginning with a drive to improve the first-call medical facilities that were available at the tracks.

Stewart failed to fulfil his early-season promise and reached the end of the season without another win. The losing trend continued to dog him in the season that followed, which turned out to be the only one in which he was not able to achieve a single victory.

Stewart rejoined Tyrrell for 1968 to drive the Matra-Ford, which he managed to cover with glory at Zandvoort in the fifth race of the season. He claimed two further successes, one at the Nürburgring, where he finished more than four minutes ahead of second-placed Graham Hill. His next best achievement was a second place in the title race in the United States Grand Prix at Watkins Glen.

The Matra-Ford dominated the following season and Stewart took full advantage of his mount, gaining six victories and securing his first championship at Monza, with another three rounds to go.

Disappointingly, the March-Ford that Stewart and Tyrrell raced in 1970 proved unreliable. This spurred Ken Tyrrell on to build a chassis of his own for the following season, and to race under his own name. Stewart was having a glorious time of it. He won six of the next 11 rounds, and was thrilled to claim his second world championship title.

Mechanical difficulties dogged his car in 1972, but he was back on form the following year, to claim a third world crown with five victories. In achieving this feat he surpassed both the previous high-water marks set by Fangio and Clark, respectively.

Although Jackie Stewart had intended to retire at the end of that season, he left the competitive scene one race earlier than planned. With the championship already within his reach, Stewart was set to drive in his 100th and final Grand Prix at Watkins Glen, USA. When François Cevert died during the practice laps, he withdrew from the field as a gesture of respect for his young team-mate.

Despite receiving substantial offers, Jackie Stewart never raced again. In 1997, the flying Scotsman re-emerged on the Formula One circuit to introduce the Stewart racing team he had set up with his son, Paul. He stayed at the helm of the firm for two years, before selling it to Ford, in 1999.

**Top right: Mario Andretti in the John Player Special Lotus, one of the most recognizable Formula One cars, talks to team owner Colin Chapman.**
**Left: Jackie Stewart raced for Matra-Ford for two years, winning nine races and claiming his first Drivers' World Championship in 1969.**

# ACHIEVEMENTS

| | |
|---|---|
| Grands Prix contested | 99 |
| Grand Prix victories | 27 |
| Pole positions | 17 |
| Podium finishes | 43 |
| World championships | 1969, 1971, 1973 |

# MARIO ANDRETTI

Born: 28 February 1940

One of Formula One's most popular drivers, whose career spanned 14 years, Mario Andretti will be best remembered for his thrilling exploits behind the wheel of the UK-based Colin Chapman's legendary Lotus machines.

Mario was born in the central Italian town of Montone. Shortly after the end of World War II, in the mid-1950s, Andretti and his family emigrated to the USA, where they settled in Nazareth, Pennsylvania. The story goes that young Mario's passion for motor racing was ignited in 1954, on a trip

After a year off from Formula One, during which he concentrated on USAC races, Mario was back for the 1974 season, this time in the Parnelli team. The move proved to be a mistake and Andretti left Parnelli early in 1976 to join Colin Chapman and his re-emerging Lotus team, for whom he claimed a victory in Japan later that year.

The following season saw Mario behind the wheel of a Lotus 78, the first of the true winged Formula One machines. Although he made a brave start, winning at Long Beach, California, as well as in Spain, France and Italy, his challenge for the world championship suffered a setback when the new Lotus also suffered teething troubles.

After five races of the 1978 season, during which Mario claimed his seventh Formula One victory in Argentina, the Lotus 78 was replaced by Chapman's Lotus 79. This was the car that introduced ground-effects technology to Formula One, utilizing a rubber skirt to seal the gap

to the Italian Grand Prix at Monza, where he was entranced by the sublime skills of Alberto Ascari, driving a Ferrari.

Andretti began his own racing career in 1959, driving the ancient Hudson he shared with his cousin Aldo, on the dirt ovals of his hometown. By 1964 he had graduated to United States Auto Club (USAC) sprint cars and Indy car races. His talent began to attract attention a year later when he made his debut at the Indy 500, gaining third place and 'Rookie of the Year' honours. Five attempts later he collected his first Indy 500 trophy, but he battled for two decades trying to repeat this feat.

By 1968, the year which marked his entrance into the world of Formula One racing at Watkins Glen in the hills of upstate New York, the young Andretti had amassed a host of honours. He had been successful in the Daytona 500, at Sebring, in two USAC championships and had had four starts in the Indy 500. Although he was in pole position driving the Lotus 49B, the latent promise of this start was not fulfilled because the car failed mechanically – a fate that was to befall him twice in 1969.

Over the next few years, Mario became one of the first Atlantic commuters, taking part in Formula One races all over the world, while living in Nazareth and racing Indy cars. In March 1970 he competed in five different races, and made his first visit to the podium in Járama, Spain, where he was placed third driving a March-Ford.

In 1971 he switched to the Ferrari team, a change that paid dividends when he won his first victory for the Prancing Horse emblem in the South African Grand Prix at Kyalami, near Johannesburg. He then piloted the Ferrari nine more times, without adding to his victory tally.

***Above:*** **Mario Andretti, in the JPS Lotus 78, leads around the Loews Hairpin at the 1978 Monaco Grand Prix. Pictured second here, Patrick Depailler won the race in the Tyrrell 008.**

***Top left:*** **Youth versus experience – Andretti during his Lotus days (left), and Andretti when driving for Newman-Haas racing in America (right).**

between the bottom of the car and the race track. This revolutionary car was able to create an area of low pressure that literally sucked it down onto the track, giving the vehicle tremendous aero grip, and allowing it to hold the road firmly, even at high speeds. This car was quick off the mark and helped Andretti to pole position, and then to victory, on its first outing at the Belgian Grand Prix at Zolder.

The Andretti-Lotus 79 combination was unstoppable and success in Spain, France, Germany and Holland put the title within his reach. In the Italian Grand Prix at Monza, only his team-mate, Ronnie Peterson, was still in contention. A tragic accident shortly after the start caused Peterson to crash. His car burst into a ball of flame and the race was red-flagged while James Hunt, Patrick Depailler and Clay Regazzoni managed to drag the injured driver out of the car.

When the race restarted, Mario, believing his team-mate to be in a satisfactory condition, raced to sixth place to earn enough points to claim the championship title. His celebration, however, was subdued, tempered by the sad news that Peterson had died from an embolism.

Despite competing on the global circuit for four more years, Andretti never won another race. When he left the Formula One scene in 1982, his racing days were far from over; he dedicated himself to Indy cars, claiming a final victory at Phoenix, Arizona, in 1993.

Andretti still lives in Nazareth and often watches his son race for the Newman-Haas Indycar team, in the Champ Car Series.

## A C H I E V E M E N T S

| | |
|---|---|
| Grands Prix contested | 128 |
| Grand Prix victories | 12 |
| Pole positions | 18 |
| Podium finishes | 19 |
| World championships | 1978 |

**Top right: Niki Lauda before and after his horrific accident during the 1976 German Grand Prix at the Nürburgring. Despite his injuries, he raced at the Italian Grand Prix just six weeks later and went on to win the championship again in 1977 and 1984.**

# N I K I   L A U D A

Born: 22 February 1949

Despite winning three world championship titles, Niki Lauda will probably be best remembered for the solitary championship that he failed to win.

Lauda was born into a wealthy Viennese family and, during his early years in racing, he made use of his family's pedigree and connections to secure the money he needed to finance his career. His racing debut was made behind the wheel of a Mini Cooper, in a 1968 hillclimb event. He went on to Formula Three and then used borrowed funds to buy a Formula Two seat at March, in the company of Ronnie Peterson. When the March deal came to an end, he moved over to BRM in 1973 and luckily, just as his revenue stream was showing signs of drying up, he was signed up by Luca di Montezemolo, to drive for Ferrari.

His first victory for the Prancing Horse marque was achieved in Spain in 1974, followed by another win at Zandvoort in Holland. For the 1975 season he was partnered by Clay Regazzoni at a time when Ferrari dominated Formula One from start to finish. Niki Lauda already had five wins under his belt when he cruised to his first world championship victory.

The fateful race on which the Austrian's fame rests took place in 1976 at the Nürburgring. Lauda, driving a Ferrari, with five wins to his credit and a comfortable 20-point lead over his closest rival, was battling with James Hunt of Britain's feisty McLaren team, for his second world

pits. He retired from the race, stating that it was sheer madness to drive in such dangerous conditions. Hunt came third in the race to snatch the world championship from Lauda by a single point.

However, in 1977, Lauda was absolutely determined to put the trauma of his accident behind him. This he accomplished by collecting three wins and his second championship title. Lauda severed his links with Ferrari and joined Bernie Ecclestone at Brabham in 1978 for two unsuccessful seasons until, in Canada in 1979, mid-way through the race weekend, he decided he had had more than enough of Formula One, and retired on the spot.

After two years away from the circuit, during which he turned his mind to promoting Lauda Air, the commercial airline he had set up, he was lured back to the sport when an offer made by Ron Dennis of McLaren proved irresistible. In his comeback year of 1982, Niki Lauda claimed two further victories, one at Long Beach and another at Brands Hatch, but he could not win a single race in 1983.

For 1984 Lauda had a new and impressively fast team-mate in Alain Prost (who took the championship in 1985), but Lauda held strong to the end for a championship-winning margin of a mere half a point.

A sole race victory in 1985, in the Dutch Grand Prix at Zandvoort, finally brought down the curtain on the illustrious career of one of motorsport's bravest and most determined heroes.

championship crown, at the awe-inspiring 23km (14-mile) old 'Ring, when things went badly wrong for Austria's star driver. Just past Bergwerk, his Ferrari inexplicably swerved violently to the right. It crashed into an embankment, spun back into the path of the oncoming cars and ricocheted back across the track, where it connected with Brett Lunger's Surtees. In an instant the car was enveloped in flames. The stricken Austrian was dragged from the cockpit by Lunger, Guy Edwards and Arturo Merzario. He sustained terrible burns to his head and body, and for a while it was uncertain whether he would survive. Miraculously he recovered and was back in the cockpit and racing within six weeks of the accident.

With this hiatus, Hunt had begun to make inroads into Lauda's commanding lead. Over the following three races, Niki Lauda was not on top of his form and his lead was further reduced to just three points. Only the Japanese Grand Prix remained to be run, but the race at Fuji began in appalling weather and, after two laps, Lauda drove his Ferrari into the

| A C H I E V E M E N T S | |
|---|---|
| Grands Prix contested | 171 |
| Grand Prix victories | 25 |
| Pole positions | 24 |
| Podium finishes | 32 |
| World championships | 1975, 1977, 1984 |

**Top left:** Niki Lauda in the Ferrari 312T leading James Hunt and Clay Regazzoni at the French Grand Prix in 1976.

**Top right:** Gilles Villeneuve (right) and McLaren driver Patrick Tambay.

**Right:** Gilles Villeneuve wrestles with the Ferrari 312T5 at the 1980 Monaco Grand Prix. The Canadian managed only six points during a difficult season.

# GILLES VILLENEUVE

Born: 18 January 1952 • Died: 8 May 1982

I n his six short years in Formula One, Gilles Villeneuve raced a mere 67 times, winning six races, but the reputation he made for himself bears little relationship to that modest record. Villeneuve's career still sparks debate among Formula One judges, more so than that of any other driver. Some were captivated by his aggressive style and never-say-die attitude, while others thought he lacked composure and the ability to handle the powerful Formula One machinery. One thing was certain, however – when Gilles Villeneuve raced you were sure to have fireworks.

Gilles Villeneuve was born on 18 January 1952 in Quebec, Canada, and spent his younger days racing snowmobiles with his friends. He was later to claim that being thrown out of a snowmobile onto the ice at about 160kph (100mph), was a pretty good preparation for the dangerous, high-speed world of Formula One racing.

Villeneuve's earliest experience of motor racing was driving for the Ecurie Canada team in the 1976 Formula Atlantic Championship. He dominated the championship, although due to a shortage of funds, he was forced to sit out a race meeting when his team could not afford to enter. In spite of his impoverished situation, he nevertheless managed to catch the eye of the McLaren team management who elevated him to Formula One.

Villeneuve made his debut at the 1977 British Grand Prix at Silverstone in the same event that saw the debut of the Renault turbo. He put in a strong performance in the McLaren M23 and, despite a pitstop and faulty oil gauge, finished 10th, two laps behind the winner, James Hunt. Though not a bad performance, McLaren boss Teddy Mayer decided not to retain Villeneuve's services, and it looked as if he would be without a car.

Three months later, after a call from Enzo Ferrari at Maranello, Villeneuve was aboard the Ferrari 312T2 for the Canadian Grand Prix. He made a less than auspicious beginning with the Italian team. At Mosport he spun out late in the race and during the next round at Fuji, Japan, disaster struck. Early on, Villeneuve's Ferrari and the Tyrrell of Ronnie Peterson made contact and spun into a group of spectators in an illegal area beside the track, killing two of them.

Villeneuve was back with Ferrari the following year, in spite of this profoundly shocking incident. Furthermore, he was able to proudly claim his

maiden Formula One victory in the final race of that year, his own home Grand Prix held at Montreal.

The 1979 season, during which he battled team-mate Jody Scheckter for the championship, was to prove Villeneuve's best. He won three races at Kyalami in South Africa and the two US Grands Prix at Long Beach and Watkins Glen. But it was not enough. Although he matched Scheckter for wins, the South African's greater reliability was enough to tip the scales in his favour – along with the benefit of team orders. Therein lies the paradox of Gilles Villeneuve: he led more laps than any other driver that year, yet failed to amass sufficient points to take the crown.

The following year was a winless affair with Ferrari trailing along in 10th spot in the Constructors' Championship with the uncompetitive 312T5. The next was not much better, although Villeneuve managed to collect two of Formula One's most memorable victories – at Monaco and Járama, Spain. Járama was to be his final taste of success in Formula One.

Gilles Villeneuve's promising career was tragically cut short when he lost his life on 8 May 1982 while qualifying for the Belgian Grand Prix at Zolder. On one last flying lap towards the end of the session, Villeneuve came across the March of Jochen Mass. The German racer attempted to move out of the way of Villeneuve's oncoming car, but only succeeded in moving in front of the Ferrari. The resulting collision sent Villeneuve cartwheeling down the track. Although he was resuscitated at the scene, he succumbed to his injuries later that evening.

## A C H I E V E M E N T S

| | |
|---|---|
| Grands Prix contested | 67 |
| Grand Prix victories | 6 |
| Pole positions | 2 |
| Podium finishes | 13 |
| World championships | None |

**Left: Gilles' son, Jacques Villeneuve, turned to Formula One racing after a successful career in Indy cars. Here he celebrates after winning the 1997 Luxembourg Grand Prix at the Nürburgring for Williams.**

# NELSON PIQUET

Born: 17 August 1952

**M**oody, temperamental, unpredictable and capricious – these words describe a man who, above all, was a fighter and a true champion.

Born in Rio de Janeiro on 17 August 1952, Piquet's early career in Brazil, though successful, went largely unnoticed until he arrived in Europe in 1977 loaded with sponsors' money and looking for a drive. He found it in the European Formula Three championship and won two races in his Ralt RT1. The following year he raced in British Formula Three, driving Greg Siddle's Ralt RT1. A season-long battle with Derek Warwick ended with the pair sharing the honours: Piquet won the BP Formula Three championship, and Warwick the Vandervell title.

The Brazilian made his Grand Prix debut at Hockenheim in 1978. Driving an Ensign-Ford Cosworth N177 for the Team Tissot Ensign Operation, he qualified 21st. The next round took place at the Osterreichring, and once again he was there, but not in an Ensign. He had been signed up in the third McLaren alongside James Hunt and Brett

*Above:* **Ayrton Senna and Nelson Piquet (right) share the podium after Piquet triumphed in the 1986 Brazilian Grand Prix. Senna finished second, making it a one-two finish for Brazil.**

*Right:* **Nelson Piquet contending with a driver's worst enemy, a wet track, in the Brabham-BMW BT54 during his final season with the Brabham team.**

Lunger, a seat he was to retain for the Austrian Grand Prix, the Dutch Grand Prix at Zandvoort, and the Italian Grand Prix at Monza.

Piquet missed the penultimate round at Watkins Glen but was back for the finale at Montreal, with his third team of the season. This time he had been snapped up by Brabham team owner Bernie Ecclestone to drive the Alfa Romeo-powered Brabham BT46, in partnership with Niki Lauda and John Watson. This was an entirely different prospect from the McLaren and Ensign which Piquet had driven earlier in the season. His performance was good enough to earn him a full-time seat alongside Niki Lauda for the 1979 campaign, only this time round the Brabham Alfas were not quite as competitive, although Piquet still qualified in the top four on six occasions.

For 1980, Piquet was with the Parmalat Brabham team, this time as the undisputed Number One, partnered by Argentinian, Ricardo Zunino. The BT49 powered by Ford Cosworth was a potent package and Piquet claimed his debut Formula One victory at Long Beach, following this up with late-season wins at Zandvoort and Monza, to gain a second place in the championship.

At the start of the 1981 season the Brazilian driver's high hopes were fulfilled when he won the third race of the season at Buenos Aires in the Gordon Murray-designed BT49C. The next outing at Imola brought yet another win, but all his work was wasted when his success was followed by three consecutive non-finishes. Things continued poorly for Piquet until a stunning drive at Hockenheim re-ignited his chances. This was to be his final

victory that year, but having picked up points regularly he was still in contention before the final round, where he finished ahead of Carlos Reutemann at Las Vegas to take the title. Of the 15 races that year, Piquet won three, was on the podium seven times and scored points in 10 for a total of 50 points, one clear of Reutemann and four ahead of Jacques Laffite.

Piquet's 1982 season was dismal, with only one victory, at Montreal. In 1983, partnered by Riccardo Patrese, the more reliable BMW turbo engine heralded good prospects for the year ahead. It began promisingly, with a victory in Brazil, but that was that until the last three races of the season. With Alain Prost in the championship lead, Piquet put together back-to-back wins and, when Prost failed to finish the final round in Kyalami, Piquet was champion again.

The next two years, his last with Brabham, brought only three wins, spread over the two seasons.

The move to Williams for 1986 rejuvenated the Brazilian, but Piquet's year-long battle with team-mate Nigel Mansell, which included four wins, merely succeeded in permitting Alain Prost to snatch the title at Adelaide, in the final race of the season.

Piquet was still with Williams for 1987, when the Williams-Honda was in winning form. Although Piquet could not match Mansell for race wins

(he scored three to the Briton's five), the points he accumulated over the season earned him his third world championship.

Little did he know that his career had reached its zenith and, aided by a poor choice of teams in his remaining seasons, he was never again to mount a challenge for the world title despite three race wins for Benetton.

## ACHIEVEMENTS

| | |
|---|---|
| Grands Prix contested | 204 |
| Grand Prix victories | 23 |
| Pole positions | 24 |
| Podium finishes | 60 |
| World championships | 1981, 1983, 1987 |

***Below:*** **It took Nigel Mansell 14 years of trying, but after some memorable failures, most notably at Adelaide in 1986, he eventually won the world championship in 1992.**

# NIGEL MANSELL

Born: 8 August 1954

*Left:* **Nigel Mansell is best remembered for his exploits behind the wheel of the Williams Renault, winning 27 races and one world championship in his six years with the team.**

The Italians call him 'Il Leone', the lion. This nickname draws together the varied components that make Nigel Mansell the formidable racer he is. It took him 14 years to achieve his ambition to win the world championship but throughout the preceding 12 seasons he thrilled his thousands of fans with his aggression, commitment and sheer force of will.

Nigel Ernest James Mansell was born on 8 August 1954 in Worcestershire, England. He was raised in the flat above the family's café and, in common with many men who achieve great things in motorsport, he first drove a car at an early age. Little did he realize what an impact that spin around a field in an Austin Seven would have on his life.

Nigel started his racing career in karts and progressed to Formula Ford, winning a championship in just his second season. His Formula One break came courtesy of Colin Chapman and he raced for Lotus 59 times between his 1980 debut at the Österreichring and his Lotus finale at Estoril in 1984, still chasing that elusive first victory.

During his career he participated in 187 races, winning 31 Grands Prix and 32 pole positions. His points haul totalled an amazing 482. Yet it looked, at one stage, as if he were destined to end his racing days without the title he craved. In 1991, after 11 years in Formula One, he prematurely

*Right:* **Mechanics work on Nigel Mansell's Williams Judd at the 1988 Spanish Grand Prix at Jeréz. The Briton finished second behind Alain Prost in the McLaren Honda.**

Five race victories at Belgium, Canada, France, Britain and Portugal left him in charge of the championship. But in the final race a tyre exploded on the street circuit at Adelaide and put paid to his dream. History was to repeat itself in 1987. Having won six victories, an accident in the penultimate round put him out of contention, and handed the title to his team-mate, Nelson Piquet.

A dismal 1988 season with the Judd V10 prompted his move to Ferrari for 1989. Victory in his debut race for Ferrari at Rio de Janeiro gave a false impression of the Ferrari 640's potential. Mansell and Gerhard Berger achieved just one victory apiece over the remainder of the season.

For the 1990 campaign it was all change, with Berger moving over to McLaren (he was replaced at Ferrari by Alain Prost). This was to be another season of bitter disappointment for Mansell with a solitary victory at Portugal to show for all his efforts.

announced his retirement after the disappointment of withdrawing his Ferrari at Silverstone in 1990. A quick call from Frank Williams persuaded him to change not only his mind, but the course of his life.

Mansell had first made the move to Williams in 1985 to join Keke Rosberg in the Honda-powered FW10. It was a while before he settled into the new role, but two victories in the last three races moved him up to sixth place in the Drivers' Championship and into a good position for 1986.

The 1986 season was the one that made Mansell a superstar in the eyes of Britain's sporting public, and it seemed as though the title would be his.

*Top left:* Watching the qualifying lap times at Silverstone in 1992.
*Bottom left:* In 1993 Mansell won the American Indycar Championship driving for the Paul Newman's Newman-Haas Team.
*Bottom right:* Mansell's famous 'red 5' Indycar in action.
*Opposite:* Mansell surprised himself and the team by winning his debut race for Ferrari, driving the Ferrari 640 at the 1989 Brazilian Grand Prix.

Mansell probably hoped that the reprieve offered by Frank Williams, and a chance to drive the Williams-Renault FW14, would give him an immediate ascendancy, but he was to be disappointed right from the start of the 1991 season. It was Ayrton Senna who assumed control with four victories in the first four races. It took some time for Mansell, Williams and Renault to get their combined act together. A run of four victories and two second places in mid-season was a very encouraging sign that a late challenge from them might be on the cards. However, their optimism was not justified.

Then came Formula One 1992, and from the first round, in the gold-fields of South Africa, it appeared as if Mansell had struck a seam of pure gold. He was the fastest all weekend, laid claim to his 18th pole position and led the race from start to finish. The rest of the season was run in much the same style and the gallant British driver scored nine race victories, which gained him the world title he had pursued for so long. After his hard-won

championship success, Mansell abandoned Williams for the American Indy-car series. Although he scored a surprising victory in 1993, he decided to leave that field, however, after a lacklustre second season. A brief flirtation with Williams (1994) and McLaren (1995) followed, before motorsport's greatest showman, 'Il Leone', quit the stage.

# A C H I E V E M E N T S

| | |
|---|---|
| Grands Prix contested | 187 |
| Grand Prix victories | 31 |
| Pole positions | 32 |
| Podium finishes | 59 |
| World championships | 1992 |

# ALAIN PROST

Born: 24 February 1955

**Left: Alain Prost must have acquired a taste for champagne with 51 victories over his 13-year Formula One career, not to mention his 76 other visits to the podium in second and third place.**

Some people dream of racing cars from an early age, but not Alain Prost. Born on 24 February 1955 in Lorette, Saint Chamond, close to St Etienne in France, where his father was the local carpenter, young Alain thought of becoming a footballer for the St Etienne team, or perhaps settling for the same trade as his father.

On a visit to Monaco for a family holiday, Alain watched in awe as Jacky Ickx won the Grand Prix. The race fired his imagination and Prost sought out his local karting track, acquired a licence and started to race.

In his early career he was thought to be no more than an average driver. He was supported by his family and did not seem to take karting seriously – he raced for fun. His attitude hardened when, in 1973, he joined the French junior karting team.

During 1975 he travelled down to Paul Ricard in his old Renault 16 to attend the Winfield Driving School. When it came to racing cars, Prost was a natural. He spent two years in Formula Three, and competed several times in Formula Two. During one of those races, Prost so impressed the watching Teddy Mayer that a contract awaited his signature at the finish.

In his debut season for Formula One, 25-year-old Prost and his partner, John Watson, in the McLaren M29 powered by a Ford Cosworth V8, collected five points. Prost's first two races were both top-six finishes.

For the next season he moved to the all-French Renault team to partner René Arnoux. Prost was immediately in the frame, scoring his debut victory in his home race, at Dijon-Prenois. He picked up further wins at Zandvoort and Monza before the end of the year.

In 1982 he was still at Renault with Arnoux and the powerful Renault RE30B-Renault V6, poised to be a force in the chase for the crown. Victories in the first two races fuelled false hopes. Prost failed to finish in any of the next seven outings. The arrival of the Renault V6 turbo in 1983 heightened expectations among the French team and their followers and

**Right: A contemplative Alain Prost before the 1993 Brazilian Grand Prix.**
**Below: Prost drives the TAG Porsche-powered McLaren MP4/2C to victory at the 1986 Monaco Grand Prix, one of his five victories in a championship-winning season.**

this time their optimism was well founded. Prost collected four victories before a blown turbo in the final race at Kyalami ended his title chase.

The time was ripe for a move and Prost returned to McLaren. With cars now powered by the TAG Porsche V6 turbo, he and his team-mate, Niki Lauda, looked set to dominate Formula One. They were not disappointed. The partners won 12 of the next 16 races, Prost winning seven to Lauda's five. Despite his apparent superiority, Prost lost the championship by half a point and, in hindsight, his nemesis may well have been the Monaco Grand Prix, where he had been forced to retire in his first three seasons.

Having lost another opportunity to win the championship, Prost was determined that 1985 would be his year. Teamed with Niki Lauda and the Porsche turbo engine, he felt invincible. A victory in the opening round was followed by triumphs at Monaco, the Österreichring, Silverstone and Monza, helping him to his first world title.

Prost was on a roll and, in 1986, he was able to take advantage of the infighting between Williams rivals Mansell and Piquet to claim a second world championship with four victories. Despite winning two of the first three races of 1987, this was not a good season for Prost. However, the next few years were some of the most talked about in Formula One history and he again claimed the championship title in 1989 and 1993.

## ACHIEVEMENTS

| | |
|---|---|
| Grands Prix contested | 199 |
| Grand Prix victories | 51 |
| Pole positions | 33 |
| Podium finishes | 127 |
| World championships | 1985, 1986, 1989, 1993 |

# D A M O N   H I L L

Born: 17 September 1960

Damon Hill was born in London, the son of legendary British driver Graham Hill (*see* page 41). Damon began his motor racing career in 1979, on two wheels in British motorcycle races, using the income from his job as a motorcycle dispatch rider to finance his career. In 1983 he took part in his first motor race at Brands Hatch, in the Formula Ford 2000 winter series.

Damon Hill's route to Formula One proved to be long and hard. His late father's illustrious career did not help and it took the younger Hill nine years and 10 seasons before he could compete at a similar level.

The years of 1984 and 1985 were spent in competition in the British Formula Ford 1600 series, where Damon had two wins at Brands Hatch as well as a 10th and a third place. Moving up to the Lucas British Formula Three championship in 1986, he managed to come a respectable ninth, making his best result a second place finish at Snetterton in Norfolk.

Hill's second year in Formula Three showed a vast improvement: he won twice that year, at Zandvoort and again at Spa. Two pole positions and two fastest laps put Damon in fifth place by the end of 1987. His third and final season with Formula Three in 1988 was to prove his most successful, and he managed to achieve a total of eight podium finishes which included

two wins, two pole positions and a fastest lap. He finished the year third overall in the Formula Three championship.

That year was a watershed for Hill. He put in two appearances behind the wheel of a Lola-Ford Cosworth in the FIA Formula 3000 championship. Over the next three years he was to compete in both the British and the International Formula 3000 series, where his best championship finish was a ninth place in 1991.

Impressed by his ability, Frank Williams gave Hill his first realistic chance to shine on the Formula One circuit, as test driver for the Williams team. In 1992 Hill was offered the opportunity he longed for – the chance to test his skills in Formula One. Both race and venue were a gift for Hill: the British Grand Prix at Silverstone.

However, the Brabham Judd he was offered was neither particularly reliable nor fast and Hill finished the race four laps behind the winner, Nigel Mansell. It had given him a tantalizing taste of things to come.

Mansell's decision to leave Formula One after claiming the 1992 title opened the way for Hill to step up to race driver, as partner to Alain Prost.

From this point on, Damon Hill's career gained real momentum. For the next four seasons he was fortunate enough to be behind the wheel of the Williams-Renault, during its spell of dominance. In a four-year period he won 21 times, from pole position on no less than 20 occasions.

The very first season with Williams was one spent learning the ropes, watching, waiting and playing second fiddle to Alain Prost while the French driver made his relentless advance towards his fourth world championship. Hill, having narrowly missed the title in 1994 and 1995 following two season-long struggles with Michael Schumacher, was to reap his reward in 1996, which proved to be a year of extremes for the patient Hill, with several euphoric high points and some desperate lows.

**Top left: After winning the world championship with Williams in 1996, Damon Hill was dropped by Williams, driving for Arrows and Jordan before retiring at the end of the 1999 season.**
**Right: Hill ponders his future at his final Formula One race at Suzuka in 1999, after a career that spanned eight years.**

On the positive side, he qualified on pole nine times, scored eight victories and won the title by 19 points from his team-mate, Jacques Villeneuve, thus becoming the first son of a world champion to become world champion. His jubilation was short lived. At Monza, before his title had even been confirmed, it was announced that he did not feature in Frank Williams' plans for the next season. The team boss had opted to retain Jacques Villeneuve and replace Hill with the German, Heinz-Harald Frentzen.

So, for 1997, Hill signed with Tom Walkinshaw and the Arrows, a team that appeared to be on the rise. But problems with the car prevented Damon from demonstrating his true form and it proved a dismal year for the new world champion.

Hill changed livery once more, signing up with Eddie Jordan's 1998 team, based at Silverstone. It was, for him, a modest improvement. He finished respectably in the points on several occasions and handed his new team its first Formula One victory at Spa-Francorchamps.

Despite this success, Damon appeared to be losing the necessary focus as his family claimed more of his time and attention. A string of lacklustre results in 1999 heralded the announcement that Hill was retiring from the sport. A truly great British sportsman, Damon Hill left the field to a new generation of drivers, having achieved a grand total of 22 wins and 42 podium finishes.

## ACHIEVEMENTS

| | |
|---|---|
| Grands Prix contested | 99 |
| Grand Prix victories | 22 |
| Pole positions | 20 |
| Podium finishes | 42 |
| World championships | 1996 |

# MIKA HAKKINEN

Born: 28 September 1968

Back-to-back world championships for Mika Hakkinen in 1998 and 1999 powered the Finn into the select band of the world's greatest drivers.

Hakkinen joins six other luminaries who have achieved this feat: Alberto Ascari (1952-53), Juan Manuel Fangio (1954-55, 1956-57), Jack Brabham (1959-60), Alain Prost (1985-86), Ayrton Senna (1990-91) and Michael Schumacher (1994-95). However, for a long time it appeared that he was destined to be yet another of the drivers whose sublime talent promised so much but whose career delivered minimal rewards.

*Above: It took Mika Hakkinen eight years to claim his first world championship, in 1998, just one year after he had won his first Formula One race.*
*Right: The West McLaren Mercedes took Mika Hakkinen to his second successive world championship in 1999.*

Mika Hakkinen was born in Vantaa near Helsinki, Finland, on 28 September 1968. He was just five when he began his racing career in karts. The 13 years he spent racing karts gave him a solid grounding in race craft as well as earning him five Finnish championships. When he moved up to Formula Ford in 1987 he scooped the Finnish, Swedish and Nordic championships before going on to gain champion status in the Opel Lotus Euroseries, and he was runner-up in the British Vauxhall Lotus challenge.

Formula Three was his next target and in 1989 he raced the Reynard-Honda of Dragon Racing to seventh place in the British Formula Three championship, the series that had spawned great racers like Ayrton Senna, Martin Brundle and David Coulthard. The following season, in the more competitive West Surrey Racing Ralt-Mugen Honda he claimed the championship, as well as winning a heat of the famous Macau Formula Three Grand Prix.

Spurning offers from top F3000 teams, Hakkinen leaped straight into Formula One in 1991 with the famous Lotus team, which at that time was cash-strapped and struggling. He raced for the Norfolk-based team for two seasons during which his best results were two fourth places (France and Hungary, 1992). Despite his lack of results, Hakkinen had impressed McLaren owner, Ron Dennis, enough to be offered a drive for 1993. The problem was that Dennis had already signed Ayrton Senna and Michael Andretti, so the Finn spent most of that year as test driver. When Andretti went back to Indycars, he stepped in for the final three races, making it to the podium in Japan.

For three years Hakkinen performed impressively in the McLaren, but despite 11 visits to the podium, he failed to gain that elusive victory. His quest to open his Formula One account faded into insignificance in Adelaide, at the season-closing Australian Grand Prix in 1995. The Finn lost control of his McLaren Mercedes during the qualifying laps and hit the barriers side on, his head making contact with the wall. For several days, Hakkinen lay in a coma, and there were doubts as to whether he would live. He did, and five months later he was back behind the wheel for the opening race of 1996. It was not one of his best years.

In 1997 he won the European Grand Prix in Jeréz, Spain, a victory owed more to team orders and the complicity of Jacques Villeneuve (who had been the race-leader) than to any real merit on Hakkinen's part.

The same could be said of his second victory at Melbourne, in the opening race of the 1998 campaign, when team-mate David Coulthard controversially slowed to allow Hakkinen to regain the lead he had lost in a fumbled pitstop. If there was a measure of good fortune in that victory, Hakkinen silenced the doubtful by reeling off another seven that year on the way to a well deserved world championship.

Hakkinen held on to his crown in 1999 with five race wins but could not defend it in 2000, losing to the powerful Schumacher/Ferrari team.

## ACHIEVEMENTS

| | |
|---|---|
| Grands Prix contested | 145 |
| Grand Prix victories | 18 |
| Pole positions | 26 |
| Podium finishes | 48 |
| World championships | 1998, 1999 |

# MICHAEL SCHUMACHER

Born: 3 January 1969

*Left:* **Michael Schumacher celebrates on the podium with the enigmatic Flavio Briatore, his team boss at Benetton during the four years that netted him 19 race wins and two world championships.**

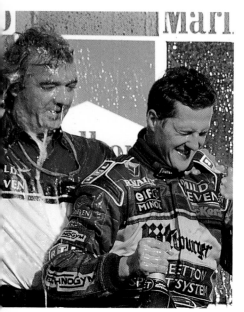

The 1994 Australian Grand Prix at Adelaide brought to a controversial climax the riveting and sometimes distasteful championship battle between Michael Schumacher in the Benetton-Ford and Damon Hill in the Williams-Renault. The German began the final race of the season one point ahead of his British rival. He needed to finish ahead of Hill or else prevent him from scoring a further point – this he achieved with a collision that took both men out of the race. Schumacher was roundly condemned from all quarters for his ruthless tactics, but when the dust had settled the fact remained: Schumacher was world champion at the age of 25.

If stars are born, not made, no extraordinary indications attended the birth of Michael to Rolf and Elisabeth Schumacher on 3 January 1969 in Hurth-Hermuhlheim, west of Cologne in an area known as the flatlands.

His interest in motor racing was sparked by a gift from his parents; four-year-old Michael was delighted with a pedal go-kart that was soon converted to power by the addition of a lawnmower engine.

Success started with the German Junior Championships of 1984 and 1985 and in the latter season, a second place at the Junior World Championship at Le Mans. In 1986 he graduated to the German Senior Championship; 1987 was destined to be Schumacher's final season in karting and a move to cars seemed the natural progression. His first season saw him race in Formula Koenig, in which he won nine of the 10 rounds on his way to the championship.

After rapidly progressing up the racing ladder Schumacher was elevated to German Formula Three for 1989. The following season he joined the Mercedes Sports Car World Championship team as part of the new Mercedes Junior team. Along with Heinz-Harald Frentzen and Karl Wendlinger he was to partner Jochen Mass.

He stayed with Mercedes for the following season but late in the year a call came from Jordan. They were short of a driver in their first season of Grand Prix racing, as their regular pilot, Bertrand Gachot, had landed in prison after an altercation with a London taxi driver.

Schumacher was impressive at Spa, qualifying in seventh position. His race lasted than less than one lap, but Benetton had seen enough to sign him to replace Roberto Moreno for the rest of the season. It was an eventful one for the bright new star of Formula One, finishing fifth at Monza and sixth at Estoril and Barcelona, before having to retire at both of the final two rounds in Japan and Australia. In his first full season with Benetton, in 1992, Schumacher trailed in the wake of the dominant Williams-Renaults driven by Mansell and Patrese, but he earned his first victory at Spa-Francorchamps, on the anniversary of his Grand Prix debut.

For the 1993 season Williams was again the team to beat and it was the same tough battle, with a solitary victory at Estoril the modest reward for some spirited driving.

Williams-Renault looked on good form for the 1994 season, with their new number one driver, Ayrton Senna. But the year could not have started better for Schumacher with victories in the first two rounds, at Interlagos, Brazil, and Aida, Japan, after Senna retired from both races. As the world looked on, round three at Imola brought the danger of Formula One motor racing harshly back into focus. Three-time world champion Ayrton Senna and newcomer Roland Ratzenberger both lost their lives. History records that Schumacher went on to win the race, and extend his lead in the championship, but on this tragic day that counted for little.

Successive wins in Montreal and Magny-Cours followed, but then fate turned against Schumacher. What had looked like a stroll to the title was severely threatened by his disqualification at Silverstone for overtaking Hill on the parade lap and then ignoring a black flag.

The German Grand Prix was once again a source of frustration, as his usually reliable Ford engine expired during the race. A victory at the Hungaroring, however, put his quest back on course.

Damon Hill gained maximum points with victories at both Monza and Estoril and the gap between him and Schumacher narrowed to one point with three rounds remaining. At Jeréz, Schumacher triumphed – then Hill won in Japan leaving it all down to the wire for the race in Australia, scene of the infamous Adelaide confrontation.

Nine wins in 1995, and a 33-point lead, gave Schumacher his second world championship. Ferrari then lured him for 1996 to chase the title that had eluded them for so long. Despite some incredible performances, the team's efforts were hampered by bad luck and costly errors. Finally, in 2000, Schumacher delivered the Drivers' and Constructors' titles to Ferrari, becoming their most successful driver in world championship events.

*Above:* The Tifosi show their excitement as Schumacher wins the 2000 San Marino Grand Prix at Imola. Ferrari dominated the early action of the new millennium and Schumacher went on to claim the Drivers' title.

## ACHIEVEMENTS

| | |
|---|---|
| Grands Prix contested | 143 |
| Grand Prix victories | 44 |
| Pole positions | 32 |
| Podium finishes | 83 |
| World championships | 1994, 1995, 2000 |

# A Y R T O N   S E N N A

Born: 21 March 1960 • Died: 1 May 1994

For some, the glittering world of Formula One motor racing was never the same after 1 May 1994, at Imola, the day Ayrton Senna died, when his Williams FW16 left the track at high speed, on a sweeping right-hander known as Tamburello.

This was the most publicized fatality in history – more people witnessed Senna's accident than had seen the assassination of President John F Kennedy. Millions of fans around the world watched in horror as the man many thought the greatest driver the sport had ever seen, lost his life.

The irony of the situation was that Senna, for the 10 years of his association with Formula One, was the last person anyone expected to die behind the wheel of a racing car. He was the ultimate performer, a driver almost uncannily in tune with his machine and his surroundings. He always appeared to be in control of events.

He was born Ayrton Senna da Silva in São Paulo, Brazil, on 21 March 1960 to Milton and Neide. The family was rich, with interests in farming and a thriving car component business, but while their wealth put young Senna at an advantage and afforded him the opportunity to drive early in life, it cannot explain the talent that he was to display in later years.

At the age of seven, Ayrton would drive a jeep around the family's farm, changing gear without the aid of a clutch. Even at this young age he was at one with the machine he drove. By the time he was 10 he had his own kart, and a powerful one at that.

In 1981 Senna moved to Europe and enjoyed two successful Formula Ford seasons before starting in Formula Three in 1983, for Dick Bennetts' West Surrey Racing team. Senna reeled off nine victories – with eight fastest laps from his first nine races – well on the way to the crown.

A mid-season test with Williams heightened Senna's desire to race in Formula One. A test drive for McLaren followed, but a better offer came from the Toleman team who asked him to drive for them.

Senna's Grand Prix debut was on his home ground in the Brazilian Grand Prix at Rio de Janeiro. He started badly, in a season beset with mechanical failures for the Toleman-Hart TG183B and TG184, but managed to earn three podium finishes and finished the season joint ninth with Mansell.

*Top left:* **A youthful Senna celebrates on the podium during his three-year stint at Lotus.**

*Left:* **The distinctive famous yellow helmet – Ayrton Senna drives the Lotus 97T to victory at Estoril in 1985.**

*Right:* **After three years at Lotus, Ayrton Senna moved to McLaren to forge an uneasy alliance with Alain Prost.**

The following year, to Toleman's chagrin, Senna jumped ship for Lotus. The three years that Senna spent with the Norfolk-based team did not bring him any closer to the championship title he coveted, but the experience taught him that he had little to fear and that, given the best equipment, he could be unbeatable.

He claimed the first of six victories for Lotus at the 1985 Portuguese Grand Prix. Monza 1987 proved a pivotal moment in Senna's Formula One career, as it was there that Ron Dennis announced that Ayrton would partner Alain Prost at McLaren for 1988, and that the team was to be powered by Honda engines. McLaren dominated that season and, with eight victories, Senna claimed his first world championship. The Brazilian was on form again with six victories in 1989. But it was a bitter affair that culminated in the collision between the team-mates at Suzuka, giving the title to Prost.

For the 1990 campaign Senna had a new team-mate in Austrian, Gerhard Berger. As far as he was concerned, this was an altogether more agreeable partnership. Prost went off to Ferrari where he remained Senna's chief rival. Freed from acrimony, Ayrton Senna raced to two

consecutive titles, winning 13 races. He was again partnered by Berger in 1992, but their McLaren MP4/6 was not expected to be a match for the Williams of Nigel Mansell and Riccardo Patrese. Although Senna extracted the maximum from his machine to win three races, this proved true.

McLaren signed up for Ford power in the 1993 season and, with the return of Berger to Ferrari, Senna had a new team-mate in American Indycar star, Michael Andretti. The Ford engine was not the highly competitive works unit that powered rival team Benetton, but a lesser spec engine, that became a bone of contention that year. Senna was

convinced that the package he was offered would not permit him to win races, so he chose to commit himself to McLaren on a race-to-race basis. He claimed five victories that year, enjoying some great duels with Prost (Williams), who took the championship ahead of Senna by 26 points. His triumphs in the season's two final races at Suzuka and Adelaide were Senna's final victories for McLaren, indeed, his last in Formula One.

In 1994 Senna moved to the all-conquering Williams team. Tragically, in his third race for them, he was killed in a horrific crash at Imola. Motor racing had lost one of its greatest champions.

**Bottom left:** There was no better track for Ayrton Senna to display his supreme car control than Monaco. Over the years, Senna won the Monaco Grand Prix six times; in the famous 1986 event, shortened due to rain, Senna was beaten by Alain Prost.

**Bottom right:** Ayrton Senna was a master of wet conditions, the treacherous track allowing his confidence and unrivaled ability to come to the fore. Here he is pictured driving for the McLaren team, for whom he won three championship titles.

## ACHIEVEMENTS

| | |
|---|---|
| Grands Prix contested | 161 |
| Grand Prix victories | 41 |
| Pole positions | 65 |
| Podium finishes | 80 |
| World championships | 1988, 1990, 1991 |

# THE TEAMS

## A TEAM SPORT THAT DEMANDS TOTAL COMMITMENT

### A R R O W S

The Arrows team was formed in 1977 by Franco Ambrosio along with ex-Shadow men Alan Rees, Jackie Oliver and Tony Southgate. Despite having competed in over 350 Grands Prix they have yet to win a race. In fact, the one bright spot in almost 25 years of Formula One was the pole position gained by Riccardo Patrese in the 1981 US West Grand Prix, at Long Beach.

The first car the team designed was deemed to have been a copy of the Shadow and so they were forced to build a replacement. There were some promising performances in that first year, but when Riccardo Patrese left the team for Brabham, things rapidly went downhill.

Towards the end of the 1980s, aided by significant sponsorship from the Japanese company, Footwork, Arrows put in some creditable performances and claimed their best championship position with 23 points and fourth place in 1988.

*Left:* **While winning drivers are the recipients of public adulation and accolades, the unsung heroes of motorsport are without doubt the hard-working members of the back-up team who ensure that there are no technical problems. Here, Colin Chapman (left) watches critically as Mario Andretti's Lotus receives the finishing touches.**

For the 1991 season the team's name was changed to Footwork and, with a works engine deal from German sportscar manufacturer, Porsche, the future looked bright. Unfortunately, the Porsche V12 proved to be overweight and underpowered and the team declined, until in 1994 Footwork withdrew and they were re-named Arrows Grand Prix International.

On the track matters did not improve and they continued to languish near the tail of the grid until Tom Walkinshaw's TWR group, famous for its exploits with the Le Mans 24-Hour winning Jaguars, bought the team early in 1996. For the following season, the line-up included reigning world champion Damon Hill. The team remains underfunded but has moved up from the rear of the grid, to run midfield.

### M I L E S T O N E S

| | |
|---|---|
| 1977: | Team formed by Ambrosio, Rees, Oliver and Southgate |
| 1978: | First points and podium |
| 1981: | Pole position at Long Beach |
| 1991: | Team renamed Footwork |
| 1996: | Bought by Tom Walkinshaw's TWR group |

# BAR

*Left:* Jacques Villeneuve in action in the team's second race, the 1999 Brazilian Grand Prix at Interlagos. He retired after 49 laps with hydraulic failure.

One of Formula One's new teams, BAR was set up as recently as 1999 by Canadian Craig Pollock, better known as manager to Jacques Villeneuve, with the financial backing of British American Tobacco (BAT). Pollock had formed the outfit two years earlier by buying the famous but sadly declining Tyrrell team. The cars were designed by Reynard, who had been successful in F3000 and Indy-cars, and fitted with engines supplied by the proven, though under-powered Supertec. It was an impressive package for a debut team and, when they added reigning world champion Jacques Villeneuve to the equation, as well as experienced men from up and down the pit-lane, they looked set to make an immediate impression. In Formula One, however, things are never that straightforward.

BAR caused a stir even before they took to the track with their two cars liveried in two different sponsors' colours. Although FIA took exception to this, the team managed to escape without receiving a single race ban.

Their first season was harder than anyone expected. The cars proved consistently fragile and only occasionally fast. In addition, the team was hindered by the early loss of Ricardo Zonta who broke his foot. Finnish star, Mika Salo, was drafted in to replace the injured Brazilian. He at least managed to put the car across the finish line at San Marino, where he came seventh. He also finished eighth in Spain, before Zonta returned to the fray.

Villeneuve put in some typically feisty performances, although he did not manage to finish a race until Belgium, where he crossed the line in 15th place.

Despite their apparent promise, the team failed to score during their debut campaign. This was quickly redressed when Villeneuve collected points in the 2000 season-opening Australian Grand Prix.

In the ultra-competitive world of Formula One the road to the top is long, steep and full of unexpected obstacles, but BAR continues to battle on with determination.

## MILESTONES

1997:  Craig Pollock buys Tyrrell team with backing from British American Tobacco

1998:  Pollock announces team will become BAR

1999:  Formula One debut, Australian GP (Villeneuve and Zonta)

*Above:* Mechanics swarm around Jacques Villeneuve's BAR during a pit-stop at the 1999 German Grand Prix.
*Right:* Michael Schumacher has been Benetton's most successful driver, winning two world championships with the British-based team.

# BENETTON

After enjoying two years of championship success with Michael Schumacher in 1994 and 1995, Benetton has slipped back into mediocrity with just a solitary win in the past five years.

After sponsoring various Grand Prix teams, clothing manufacturer Benetton joined Formula One in its own right in 1986, when it bought the Toleman team. Gerhard Berger won the Mexican Grand Prix for the team in its first season. Benetton was also one of the few teams to mount a challenge to the dominant McLarens in 1988.

The 1989 season marked the start of a new era with charismatic businessman Flavio Briatore joining the outfit. Despite his scant knowledge of motorsport, the Italian made some shrewd decisions, forming technical partnerships, first with John Barnard and then with Tom Walkinshaw. He also had a good eye for drivers, hiring Nelson Piquet and striving to secure the services of Michael Schumacher in 1991.

The young German was an inspired acquisition and it soon became clear just how talented he was. With the Benetton improving all the time it looked as if it would become a regular winner.

The ultimate prize came in 1994, when Schumacher took the Drivers' Championship in the Ford V8-powered B194, in a year that was fraught with accusations of rule infractions and disqualifications. The German repeated the feat with Renault V10 power the following year, adding Benetton's first Constructors' Championship for good measure. Unfortunately for Benetton, Schumacher was lured away by the money, prestige and challenge of driving for Ferrari, and Benetton has been struggling to regain its prominence ever since.

Early in the 2000 season the team was purchased by Renault. This heralded the return of the enthusiastic Flavio Briatore, and it remains to be seen whether he can turn the team's fortunes.

## MILESTONES

1986: Toleman F1 purchased and renamed Benetton; First Grand Prix win in Mexico City with Berger

1994: Schumacher world champion

1995: Schumacher world champion; Constructors' champions

# BRABHAM

*Left:* Jack Brabham won the world championship for the third time in 1967, the first victory for the eponymous team.

Brabham, once a successful team, has now faded from the Formula One scene. The team was formed by double world champion Jack Brabham in 1962, but it was two years before it claimed its first victory at Rouen, where Dan Gurney had the first of two winning drives in the Brabham-Climax.

The advent of the new 3-litre category in 1966 offered the team its big break; while other manufacturers struggled with new and untried engines, Brabham opted to base its challenger on the Oldsmobile-based Repco V8 engine. In the hands of engine-tuner John Judd, the V8 proved reliable, although slightly low on power, and as the competition floundered, Brabham was able to dominate.

Over the next two seasons Brabham won eight races and claimed two Constructors' Championships along with both drivers' titles, one each for Denny Hulme and for Jack Brabham himself.

Although further race victories followed (Brabham took his tally for the team to seven, and Jacky Ickx enjoyed some success as well), the team lost its position as a dominant force in Formula One.

When he retired from driving in 1970, Jack Brabham sold his shares in the team to his partner Ron Tauranac and, apart from four wins by Carlos Reutemann and one for Carlos Pace in the mid-1970s, Brabham did not recover the mastery of earlier days.

The turnabout came under the management of Bernie Ecclestone and, more importantly, driver Nelson Piquet. The Brazilian claimed 13 race wins in seven years, winning the drivers' crown in 1981 and 1983. His departure in 1985 signalled the end of the outfit's competitiveness. Piquet's last victory for Brabham at Paul Ricard, France, in 1985 was the team's final triumph and, although it raced on until mid-1992, it was but a pale shadow of the formerly great team.

## MILESTONES

1962: Brabham formed by Jack Brabham and Ron Tauranac

1964: First Grand Prix win at Rouen with Gurney

1966: Brabham world champion; Constructors' champions

1967: Hulme world champion; Constructors' champions

1981: Piquet world champion

1983: Piquet world champion

1985: Piquet – final victory at Paul Ricard

*Below:* Nelson Piquet won 13 races in his seven years behind the wheel of a Brabham.

# F E R R A R I

**Left: One of Formula One's most enigmatic owners, Enzo Ferrari, led the Scuderia until his death, aged 90, in 1988.**

The charismatic allure of the scarlet Ferrari is universally recognized and envied. The racing team was founded by Enzo Ferrari shortly after World War II and the famous Prancing Horse marque has the distinction of being the only team to still manufacture both chassis and engines. The Scuderia scored Ferrari's first Grand Prix win in 1951. Since then race victories have come regularly. In recent years, however, Ferrari has not challenged for the championships as often as a team with its immense resources demands.

In the early days of the world championship, titles came easily to the Italian giant: two in consecutive years for Alberto Ascari in 1952 and 1953, followed by a third from Fangio three years later.

Despite winning the drivers' championships, Ferrari had to wait until 1961 to claim its first constructors' crown, the same year that Phil Hill added to its growing tally of drivers' titles.

Ferrari's other drivers' titles were earned by Mike Hawthorn, John Surtees, Niki Lauda (twice) and South African, Jody Scheckter. The latter's 1979 victory, however, proved to be the end of Ferrari's run of success for two decades until Schumacher clinched the 2000 title. While a host of great drivers such as Gerhard Berger, Alain Prost and Nigel Mansell, have subsequently tried and failed to bring glory back to Maranello, there can be little doubt that a title would have been secured in 1982 had Gilles Villeneuve not been tragically killed at Zolder.

**Below: Michael Schumacher moved from a successful career at Benetton to help Ferrari in its quest to bring the drivers' crown back to Maranello.**

When team founder Enzo Ferrari died in 1988, his beloved team came under new management. After several lean years, Jean Todt, previously of Peugeot, was hired to restore order. Results continued to be poor, but Todt worked steadily to transform Ferrari back to a dominant force. For 1996 the team acquired the services of the world's leading driver, Michael Schumacher, and as each year passed it continued to regain form and edge closer to the title it had coveted for so long, Schumacher finally taking the honours in 2000.

*Below:* **Schumacher suffered a broken leg in an accident at Silverstone in 1999 that put paid to his championship challenge, but he returned later in the season to aid team-mate Eddie Irvine's title ambitions.**

# M I L E S T O N E S

1950:    First Grand Prix team formed

1951:    First race win – British Grand Prix at Silverstone

1952/3: Ascari world champion

1956/8: Fangio/Hawthorn world champions

1961:    Hill world champion; Constructors' champions

1975/6: Lauda world champion/Constructors' champions

1977:    Lauda world champion; Constructors' champions

1979:    Scheckter world champion; Constructors' champions

1982/3: Constructors' champions

1988:    Enzo Ferrari dies        1999: Constructors' champions

2000:    Schumacher world champion; Constructors' champions

# JORDAN

*Left:* **In less than a decade, Eddie Jordan has managed to guide the Silverstone-based team to a position that challenges the sport's elite. Here, he and Damon Hill are depicted at a press conference during the 1997 Austrian Grand Prix.**

Jordan was once regarded as a team of talented enthusiasts striving to compete with larger and better financed teams, but over the decade it has competed in Formula One its stature has grown year by year.

In 1999 Jordan even had an outside shot at the driver's championship when Heinz-Harald Frentzen was still challenging for the drivers' title with three races to go.

Jordan arrived on the Formula One scene in 1991. In its first season it surprised spectators with the performances of Andrea de Cesaris and Bertrand Gachot in the eye-catching 7-Up Jordan. Jordan even found time in this busy debut season to offer a first race to a talented newcomer by the name of Michael Schumacher.

The lack of competitive engines hampered Jordan's efforts – first with the Ford V8, then an unreliable works Yamaha V12, and finally Brian Hart's underfinanced and underpowered V10.

Another works engine deal in 1995 (this time from Peugeot) and the arrival in 1996 of significant sponsorship from Benson & Hedges, increased expectations for Jordan's drivers, young Rubens Barrichello and the experienced Martin Brundle.

Team owner Eddie Jordan tried several driver combinations, such as a bold pairing of the youngsters Ralf Schumacher and Giancarlo Fisichella for 1997, followed by former world champion Damon Hill in 1998. Neither had the desired effect, although Hill did earn the team its debut victory in the 1998 Belgian Grand Prix (Spa-Francorchamps).

*Above:* **Damon Hill brought Jordan its debut victory, but failed to live up to the team's expectations during his two years with them.**

# MILESTONES

1980: Eddie Jordan retires and forms Eddie Jordan Racing

1991: Formula One debut, US Grand Prix in Phoenix

1994: Barrichello claims team's debut pole position

1998: Sign former world champion Damon Hill;

      Hill secures debut victory at Spa-Francorchamps

# LOTUS

*Left:* **The death of Colin Chapman, founder of Lotus, in 1982 was a blow from which the team never really recovered.**

The Lotus Engineering company was founded by Anthony Colin Bruce Chapman on 1 January 1952, as a direct result of his success in building and racing trials cars. The company, based finally at Ketteringham Hall, Norfolk, flourished for nearly 40 years and is remembered for introducing several groundbreaking changes that altered the face of Formula One.

Lotus made its Formula One debut in 1958 at the Monaco Grand Prix, where two years later Stirling Moss earned Lotus its first victory. Jim Clark brought the team further success with its first world title in 1963.

Although Team Lotus is best known for its involvement in Formula One, there are few circuit formulae in which the team has not triumphed in past years. In the 1950s, Lotus sports cars dominated their class in the classic Le Mans 24-Hour race, while in the mid-1960s the Indianapolis 500 race became another prize to fall to the team, along with three Grand Prix Constructors' championships. In the 1970s Lotus maintained its winning ways, collecting four Constructors' Championships, the last with the aid of the revolutionary Type-79 car.

Colin Chapman had a profound influence on the design of the Grand Prix car in post-war years. Lotus initiated development programmes that led to innovative cars with features such as monocoque construction, four-wheel-drive and ground-effects technology. Tragically, Chapman's death in 1982 from natural causes coincided with and overshadowed the development of active suspension. Lotus also introduced commercial sponsorship to Formula One in 1968 with its pioneering involvement with Imperial Tobacco.

In the 1980s Lotus entered a period of decline and Senna moved to McLaren. By 1995 the once-great team had left Formula One – a sad and premature end to an important chapter in Grand Prix history.

## MILESTONES

| | |
|---|---|
| 1958: | Lotus enters first Grand Prix, Monaco |
| 1960: | First Grand Prix victory in Monaco with Stirling Moss |
| 1961: | First victory for works team – Innes Ireland, USA GP |
| 1963: | Clark world champion; Constructors' champions |
| 1965: | Lotus Type 38 is first British car to win Indianapolis 500; Clark world champion |
| 1968: | Graham Hill world champion; Constructors' champions |
| 1970: | Rindt world champion; Constructors' champions |
| 1972: | Fittipaldi world champion; Constructors' champions |
| 1973: | Constructors' champions |
| 1978: | Andretti world champion; Constructors champions |
| 1982: | Colin Chapman dies |
| 1994: | Final season in Formula One |

*Left:* **During its 37 years in Formula One, Lotus competed in 491 races, winning 79 of them. They also had much success at Indianapolis.**

*Opposite top right:* **The founder, Bruce McLaren, died tragically in a testing accident in 1970, before his team's rise to eminence.**

*Right:* **Mika Hakkinen and the McLaren team celebrate the Finn's world championship in 1998.**

# M c L A R E N

*Left:* Ron Dennis has overseen McLaren's rise to become one of the most successful teams in Formula One history.

After dominating in the late 1980s and early 90s, the McLaren team suffered several seasons in the doldrums before returning in spectacular fashion – by taking both the Drivers' and Constructors' championships in 1998, and another drivers' title in the following year – to establish a perch at the top of Formula One's pecking order.

Founded by New Zealander Bruce McLaren in 1963, the team produced its first Grand Prix car in 1966. McLaren's first win came in 1968 at the Belgian Grand Prix, with Bruce McLaren himself at the wheel. When he was killed testing a Can Am car at Goodwood two years later, control of the team passed to one of his partners, Teddy Mayer, who continued to be moderately successful with drivers such as Denny Hulme and Peter Revson.

In 1974, McLaren won its first world championship with Emerson Fittipaldi. The team also began its long-running association with its sponsor, Marlboro. In 1976, James Hunt took the team's second

world title, following a titanic battle with the Ferrari of Niki Lauda.

In 1980, after several lean years, McLaren merged with Ron Dennis' Project Four to form McLaren International. The next year at Silverstone, John Watson took an MP4 to its first win, which was McLaren's 25th. It was also the first Grand Prix win for an all-carbon-fibre chassis.

McLaren dominated the decade, boosting its tally of Constructors'

titles to seven and Drivers' Championships to nine. McLaren was aided by drivers like Niki Lauda, Alain Prost and Ayrton Senna, as well as the engines of TAG Porsche and Honda. The team's finest hour was the season of 1988 when the two leading drivers of the era, Ayrton Senna and Alain Prost, won 15 out of the 16 races in McLaren-Hondas.

After a third world championship for Senna in 1991, the team struggled and lost the much-vaunted Honda engine when the marque pulled out of Formula One in 1992. Several seasons of struggle followed, first with Ford and then Peugeot engines, before the deal with Mercedes in 1995 propelled McLaren back among the winners.

# M I L E S T O N E S

1963: Team formed by Bruce McLaren

1966: F1 Debut in Monaco Grand Prix, M2B driven by McLaren

1968: First Grand Prix win at Belgian Grand Prix with McLaren

1970: Bruce McLaren dies, Teddy Mayer takes over

1974: Fittipaldi world champion; Constructors' champions

1976: James Hunt world champion

1980: McLaren merges with Ron Dennis' Project Four to form McLaren International

1982: Ron Dennis becomes sole principal

1984: Lauda world champion; Constructors' champions

1985: Prost world champion; Constructors' champions

1986: Prost world champion

1988: Senna world champion; Constructors' champions

1989: Prost world champion; Constructors' champions

1990: Senna world champion; Constructors' champions

1991: Senna world champion; Constructors' champions

1998: Hakkinen world champion; Constructors' champions

1999: Hakkinen world champion

**Opposite top: Johnny Herbert and Rubens Barrichello, with the Stewart-Ford team, celebrate first and third place at the 1999 European Grand Prix. Opposite bottom: The Stewart-Ford team won just one race in its three years in Formula One, Johnny Herbert's victory at the Nürburgring in 1999.**

# P R O S T

**Left: Four-time world champion, Alain Prost, has found it much tougher as a team owner than he did as a driver.**

Ligier, a sports car team created by former racer Guy Ligier in 1969, took the step up to Formula One in 1976. It is known as the 'French team', which has helped it secure sponsorship in France.

In its formative years, Ligier showed great promise, winning its first race in its second season with Jacques Laffite at the 1977 Swedish Grand Prix at Anderstorp. In 1979 Laffite won two races on his way to fourth place in the Drivers' Championship, and his teammate Patrick Depailler added a third, moving the team up to third place in the Constructors' Championship.

The following year went even better for them: Laffite was fourth again in the Drivers' Championship with 34 points, while Didier Pironi was two points behind. That year, Ligier finished second in the Constructors' rankings, behind the dominant Williams team. Although it finished fourth in 1981 with 44 points, this time all from Laffite, it had achieved its moment of glory. The team had to wait 15 years to achieve its next Formula One success, this time at the hands of Olivier Panis at Monaco in 1996.

In 1997, four-time world champion, Alain Prost, took over and renamed the team. Despite looking promising, the team has struggled on the track.

# M I L E S T O N E S

1976: Grand Prix debut in Brazil

1977: First Grand Prix win in Sweden with Laffite

1993: Cyril de Rouvre takes over from Guy Ligier

1994: Flavio Briatore takes over from De Rouvre, bringing in Tom Walkinshaw

1996: Panis wins at Monaco

1997: Alain Prost buys the team

# JAGUAR

Today known as Jaguar, the original Stewart-Ford team made an inauspicious start to its Formula One career in the 2000 season. After a high-profile launch and the signing-on of Eddie Irvine, who narrowly missed bringing the world championship back to Maranello, the team's on-track performances have been little short of disastrous, even though Jackie Stewart has been involved in motor racing management for many years.

With extensive backing from Ford, Stewart took the plunge and entered the top-ranking motorsport category for the 1997 season with drivers Rubens Barrichello of Brazil, and Jan Magnussen of Denmark. Results were hard to come by in Alan Jenkins' untried car and the team ended its debut season in ninth place with just six points. The promise was not fulfilled in 1998 and Magnussen was replaced in mid-season by Jos Verstappen.

Johnny Herbert was drafted in for the 1999 season, to partner Barrichello. The team led its first race (Barrichello in Brazil) and earned podium finishes at Imola and Magny-Cours before Herbert rounded off the season with the team's debut victory in the European Grand Prix at the Nürburgring.

Late in the season, Ford decided to buy the team from Jackie Stewart and announced the formation of Jaguar for the 2000 season.

# MILESTONES

1997: Formula One debut in Australia

1999: First Grand Prix win;
Ford buys team and renames it Jaguar

# TYRRELL

*Left:* **Team owner Ken Tyrrell offers a few words of advice to his driver, Jackie Stewart.**

Tyrrell was one of the most successful teams of the 1970s and early 1980s. After its race victory at the hands of Michele Alboreto at Detroit in the 1983 US East Grand Prix, however, it competed in 237 races without securing another win. By the end of the 1998 season, when it was bought by Craig Pollock to form BAR, it was among the perennial backmarkers. In truth, much of Tyrrell's early success can be attributed to one man: Jackie Stewart won 15 of the team's 23 victories, all in its first three years.

Ken Tyrrell's team made its debut at Mont-Tremblant in the 1970 Canadian Grand Prix. Jackie Stewart claimed pole position in the Tyrrell 001, powered by a trusty Ford Cosworth V8, but as in the other two races Tyrrell entered that year, the car failed to make it to the chequered flag.

It was a different story altogether in 1971, with Stewart claiming the world title and the team earning the Constructors' title in its first full season. It proved difficult to keep up the momentum of such a successful start and the team never won another Constructors' title over the 27 years it raced. Although Stewart did claim a second world title for the team in 1973, only four other drivers won races for Tyrrell: Jody Scheckter (four), Michele Alboreto (two) and François Cevert and Patrick Depailler one each.

## MILESTONES

1970:   Team enters Formula One;
        Pole position in debut Grand Prix, Mont-Tremblant, Canada
1971:   First Grand Prix victory in Spain;
        Stewart world champion; Constructors' champions
1973:   Stewart world champion
1983:   Alboreto scores Tyrrell's final victory
1998:   Final Grand Prix at Suzuka, Japan. Tyrrell sold to Craig
        Pollock who closed team down and started BAR

*Opposite top:* **Team boss Frank Williams flanked by his 1993 driver line-up of Damon Hill (left) and Alain Prost.**
*Below:* **Jody Scheckter in the six-wheel Tyrrell. Scheckter won four races for the team during his three-year spell with Tyrrell.**

# WILLIAMS

There is little doubt that, in recent years, Williams has been the team to beat, with its four Drivers' and five Constructors' titles since 1991. In the early days of the team, things did not go so smoothly.

Frank Williams first tried to break into Formula One in the late 1960s, but lack of financial support made success difficult to achieve. A short, ineffectual collaboration with Walter Wolf left Williams on his own again for 1977. The late 1970s, when Patrick Head was hired as designer and major backing came from Saudi Airlines, proved pivotal for him.

Clay Regazzoni claimed the team's first win at Silverstone in 1979, followed by a Drivers' Championship for Alan Jones and a Constructors' title in 1980. A second Constructors' Championship came in 1981, and another Drivers' crown for Keke Rosberg in 1982.

Honda turbo power arrived in 1984 and, after a few years of adjustment, the partnership flourished. Mansell and Piquet dominated in 1986, even though Prost claimed the championship. This despite the trauma of Frank Williams' road accident which left him paralysed.

The partnership with Honda ended with the 1987 season and, after a disappointing year with the underpowered Judd V8, Williams began another significant partnership, this time with Renault.

Williams lured Mansell out of retirement to challenge for the title in 1991, but it came up short. It was vindicated in 1992 as the Williams was dramatically faster than the opposition, allowing Mansell to cruise to the title. Alain Prost had his turn to drive the Williams in 1993 and rewarded the team with a further world championship title.

Frank Williams realized a dream when he signed Ayrton Senna, but it turned into a nightmare when the brilliant Brazilian driver was killed at Imola. This loss left Damon Hill in the driving seat. Despite Williams' dominant form, it took Hill until 1996 to win the title – and then he left to join the Arrows team. Hill's ex-team-mate, Jacques Villeneuve, won the championship for Williams in 1997.

While the departure of Renault after the 1997 season left the Williams team floundering in midfield obscurity, another significant partnership with a major motor manufacturer, this time BMW, has given the team a boost for the 2000 season.

# MILESTONES

1970: Fielded new De Tomaso for Piers Courage, who was killed in an accident at Zandvoort

1975: Merged with Walter Wolf Racing. Frank Williams left in September and started Williams GP Engineering in 1977

1979: First Grand Prix win at Silverstone with Clay Regazzoni

1980: Jones world champion; Constructors' champions

1981: Constructors' champions

1982: Rosberg world champion

1986: Constructors' champions

1987: Piquet world champion; Constructors' champions

1992: Mansell world champion; Constructors' champions

1993: Prost world champion; Constructors' champions

1994: Constructors' champions

1996: Hill world champion; Constructors' champions

1997: Villeneuve world champion; Constructors' champions

# EUROPE

## THE BIRTHPLACE OF FORMULA ONE GRAND PRIX RACING

Although Formula One races have been held at such diverse and exotic locations around the globe as Malaysia, South Africa, Brazil, Mexico and Argentina, the soul of racing still lies deep within the European heartland.

Europe is where motor racing originated and France is still home to the Fédération Internationale de l'Automobile (FIA), the sport's governing body. With few exceptions over the years, all teams have been based in Europe and this is where the innovation, the new technology and the bulk of the workforce comes from.

Around 450 (almost 70 per cent) of the races held during the first 50 years of the world championship competition took place on European circuits. To appreciate the significance of this total one only has to count the number of tracks that have hosted the most races to discover that Montreal, the first non-European track mentioned, appears only eighth on the list, having hosted 21 races. It is closely followed by Watkins Glen, Kyalami and Buenos Aires with 20 each.

*Left:* **The aerial view of Silverstone highlights the circuit's heritage — the World War II runways are clearly evident.**
*Previous pages:* **The massive crowd at Brands Hatch awaits the start of the British Grand Prix. The Kent track last hosted a round of the world championship in 1986.**

The most visited European track, the historic and beautiful Monza circuit, has hosted a race every year (excluding 1980) since the world championship started in 1950. Just one race behind Monza comes the jewel in the crown of Formula One: Monaco.

Other memorable names, both past and present, make up the top seven tracks. The scenic Spa-Francorchamps circuit through Belgium's Ardennes Forest has hosted 34, and Britain's ex-airbase, Silverstone, 33 Grands Prix. Zandvoort in the Netherlands' coastal dunes has recorded 30 world championship meetings, and the German tracks a total of 52 (the Nürburgring in both its guises a total of 29, and Hockenheim 23).

If anything can wrest control of Formula One from Europe, it will be the imminent ban on tobacco advertising, together with the attitude of the European Economic Community (EEC) towards the perceived injustice of Formula One's TV rights monopoly, negotiated by Bernie Ecclestone. Should the decisions on these matters go against Formula One, it might well be driven away from its roots into the willing arms of the Far East or South America, with Korea, India, Argentina, South Africa and China anxious to add their names to motor racing's roll of honour as a permanent fixture.

Formula One can certainly survive without Europe, but the loss of such famous and well-loved tracks would be a bitter blow indeed.

# SILVERSTONE

*Left:* David Coulthard shares the podium with Eddie Irvine and Ralf Schumacher at the 1999 British Grand Prix at Silverstone.

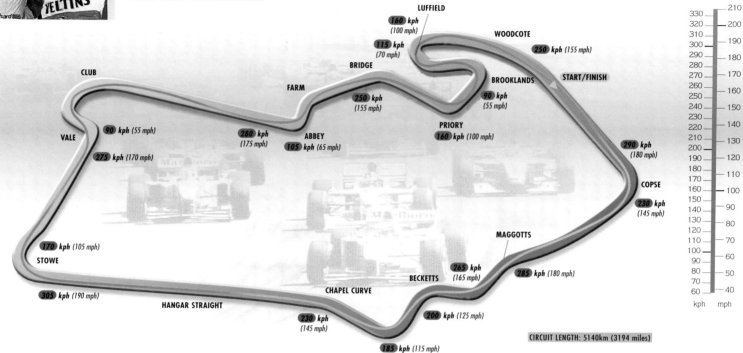

LUFFIELD
**160** *kph*
*(100 mph)*

WOODCOTE

**115** *kph*
*(70 mph)*

**250** *kph (155 mph)*

BRIDGE

CLUB

FARM

BROOKLANDS      START/FINISH

**250** *kph*
*(155 mph)*

**90** *kph*
*(55 mph)*

VALE

**90** *kph (55 mph)*

**280** *kph*
*(175 mph)*

ABBEY

PRIORY

**160** *kph (100 mph)*

**290** *kph*
*(180 mph)*

**275** *kph (170 mph)*

**105** *kph (65 mph)*

COPSE

**230** *kph*
*(145 mph)*

**170** *kph (105 mph)*

STOWE

MAGGOTTS

**265** *kph*
*(165 mph)*

BECKETTS

**285** *kph (180 mph)*

**305** *kph (190 mph)*

CHAPEL CURVE

HANGAR STRAIGHT

**230** *kph*
*(145 mph)*

**200** *kph (125 mph)*

CIRCUIT LENGTH: 5140km (3194 miles)

**185** *kph (115 mph)*

330 — 210
320 — 200
310
300 — 190
290 — 180
280
270 — 170
260
250 — 160
240 — 150
230
220 — 140
210
200 — 130
190
180 — 120
170 — 110
160 — 100
150
140 — 90
130 — 80
120
110 — 70
100
90 — 60
80 — 50
70
60 — 40

kph    mph

# GREAT BRITAIN

If France can claim to be the mother of motor racing, Great Britain was the proud father who nurtured it as it grew. For the past 40 years Britain has been the spiritual home of motorsport and many leading lights of modern Formula One are based here: McLaren, Williams, Benetton, Jordan, BAR and Jaguar.

Getting the sport established was no easy matter. Brooklands, the world's first purpose-built motor racing facility, opened in 1907 when road racing was frowned upon in the UK. As a result, Britain's motorsport had previously been confined to hill climbs and sprints.

Before World War II, Brooklands, Crystal Palace and Donington Park were the prime venues. After the war, when money was scarce, the racing community turned to disused airfields. First to open, in 1946, was Gransden Lodge followed by long-forgotten names such as Brough, Crimond, Boreham, Marston Moor and Rufforth. Then there were the survivors: Silverstone, Goodwood, Croft, Snetterton, Thruxton, Castle Combe and Oulton Park, an old army base. Of these, only Silverstone flourished. It became home to the British Grand Prix.

**SILVERSTONE:** To reach Silverstone, you drive through leafy lanes that twist their way lazily through the Northamptonshire countryside.

*Top:* The Silverstone circuit is renowned for its range of pace and, as such, is heavy on brake systems. The line on the diagram shows the ideal route and the colours denote approximate speeds.

You pass charming villages with names like Lillingstone Lovell, Whittlebury, Wappenham and Biddlesden that boast quaint Cotswold stone cottages, village shops and traditional pubs.

In contrast to other Grand Prix locations, everything about Silverstone is understated. It lacks the nostalgia of Monza and sweeping majesty of Spa, nor does it possess the urban sophistication of Barcelona, passion of Imola or glamour of Monaco. Silverstone is a racer's racing circuit without thrills or added attractions. The flat, featureless arena does not hide its past – it still looks like a World War II airstrip. The fact that Silverstone has survived for so long as Great Britain's premier circuit says something about its quality as a racetrack. What it lacks in charisma, it makes up for in the track itself and the fast, flowing layout is a test of man and machine.

When modern Formula One world championships began in 1950, Silverstone was one of the original tracks and, having been developed in 1948, a comparatively new one at that. The venue was leased from the Ministry of Defence by the Royal Automobile Club (RAC), but when it gave up the lease in 1951 it was taken over by the British Racing Drivers' Club (BRDC) to whom it still belongs. The original track – laid out on the runway – was basically the same as today. When the Silverstone circuit required improvements to both track and facilities, the BRDC took the plunge and bought it in 1961. Over the years, changes have come thick and fast: a chicane was added at Woodcote in the mid-1970s, and a new stadium complex some 20 years after that.

Silverstone had the honour of hosting the first world championship race under the title 'Grand Prix of Europe' and George VI, then Britain's reigning monarch, was there to watch Nino Farina drive the dominant Alfa Romeo to victory.

The 1951 race was significant because it saw the first-ever victory awarded to Grand Prix racing's most famous manufacturer, Ferrari. José Froilan Gonzalez, the Pampas Bull, claimed the honour and managed to do so again in 1954. These two victories at Silverstone were the Argentinian's only successes in his 10-year career.

**Right: The pageantry that preceded the start of the 1999 British Grand Prix. The race was won by David Coulthard, but blighted by the first-lap accident that left Michael Schumacher with a broken leg.**

Alain Prost was the most successful Silverstone racer of the 1980s, winning three times. In 1983, driving the Renault RE40, he came home 20 seconds clear of the Brabham of Nelson Piquet. Two years

later he won again, this time driving the McLaren MP4/2B, a whole lap clear of second-placed Michele Alboreto in a Ferrari. Still in a McLaren, he achieved his hat-trick with victory in the last race of the decade, beating local hero Nigel Mansell by 19 seconds. The Frenchman followed this success with another two victories, in a Ferrari in 1990 and a Williams in 1993, and went on to win the championship in three of the years in which he had been victorious at Silverstone.

Williams dominated the 1990s at Silverstone, with Mansell's back-to-back victories opening the decade, followed by Prost in 1993 and Damon Hill the year after that. In winning the 1994 race, Damon achieved what his father, Graham, had striven in vain to accomplish during his 18-year Formula One career: to win on home ground. Much to the delight of English fans, there was a further British success the following year, when Johnny Herbert broke the Williams run with his first Grand Prix victory in a Benetton Ford. Then it was back to Williams, with Jacques Villeneuve achieving what had eluded his

famous father, Gilles. He won the British Grand Prix in 1996, a feat he was to repeat a year later.

**AINTREE:** In 1955 the race moved north to Aintree near Liverpool. The track was a fast, flat and featureless 4.8km (3-mile) circuit running alongside the famous racecourse where the Grand National steeplechase event is held. The opening race at Aintree was the scene of one of Formula One's great finishes, with Stirling Moss taking on and beating his Mercedes team-mate, Juan Manuel Fangio. Two years later, when the race returned to Liverpool, it marked the birth of the British domination of racing with the first victory for a British-built car, the Vanwall.

*Top:* In soaking conditions Ayrton Senna started overtaking the cars in front of him to lead the race by the end of the first lap on his way to victory in the 1993 European Grand Prix at Donington Park.
*Right:* The first corner at France's Paul Ricard racetrack.

**BRANDS HATCH:** From 1964 to 1986 Silverstone shared one annual Grand Prix fixture with Brands Hatch in Kent. Originally a motor-cycling bowl, the track was paved in 1949 in its shorter Indy format and, although a very popular circuit, it proved to be far too dangerous for Formula One. Several improvements were undertaken – the track was extended in the early 1950s, the direction of racing changed to clockwise and, in 1955, a permanent grandstand was constructed. In 1964 the Kent circuit attracted its first Grand Prix – 13 more were to follow (alternating with Silverstone), until the big race reverted to Northamptonshire for good in 1987.

Brands Hatch has seen some truly excellent races: Jim Clark was the winner of the first one, held in 1964. Four years later Jo Siffert and Chris Amon put on a great show, and in 1972 there was an epic contest between Jackie Stewart and Emerson Fittipaldi.

Unfortunately, the circuit also suffered its tragedies and Jo Siffert lost his life on the sweeping right-handed, downhill corner, Paddock Hill Bend, in a start-line pile-up in 1971. Although improvements were made, safety concerns were one of the main reasons why the race returned to Silverstone for good 15 years later.

Since Brands Hatch dropped from the scene after the 1986 race, Silverstone has played host to British Formula One. Despite efforts from Brands Hatch to lure the race back to Kent, it looks set to remain at Silverstone for the foreseeable future.

**DONINGTON PARK:** The fourth British track that can claim the distinction of having held a Grand Prix is Donington Park in Leicestershire, where the European Grand Prix was run in 1993.

Situated in the grounds of 17th-century Donington Hall, it was Britain's premier racing circuit before falling into disrepair before World War II.

Tom Wheatcroft, a builder by trade, bought the track in 1971 and added the superb Donington Collection Grand Prix Car Museum in 1973. The track reopened for racing in 1977, following the lines of the original track before the Grand Prix loop was added in 1985. After many years of applying for a Grand Prix without success, Wheatcroft finally realized his ambition in 1993, albeit with just a one-off visit to the track. Ayrton Senna won the race in one of the best drives of his career.

# FRANCE

Despite France's 50-year association with motor racing, the French Grand Prix has always lacked a spiritual home. It has wandered, like a nomad, from north to south putting down temporary roots in no fewer than seven different locations. It took until the 1990s and the arrival of Magny-Cours for the race to settle down and develop a character. All the same, it is a pity that the track which it now calls home should be the least inspiring of the six that preceded it.

The French Grand Prix, along with that of Britain, Monaco, Belgium, Switzerland and Italy, claims the distinction of having been among the original six European races in the inaugural Formula One season (the seventh was the Indianapolis 500 in the USA).

While Britain sees itself as the home of modern motor racing, the sport originated in France. Today, the headquarters of the Federation Internationale de l'Automobile is still in Paris.

The very first French motor race was run between Paris and Rouen in 1894, and in the following year the Automobile Club de France (ACF) was established. During the early 20th century it was the French who built the world's superior racing machines: the Mors, Richard-Brasier, Lorraine-Dietrich and Turcat-Mery among them.

**REIMS:** The first French Grand Prix was held at Reims-Gueux, a classic circuit made famous in the 1920s. It utilized the public roads around the chief provincial town of the Champagne region. Originally called Reims-Gueux after the village of Gueux the race passed through, it became known simply as Reims when the circuit was diverted around the village after the first two races.

The first of these, held in 1950, was a no-contest dominated by Alfa Romeos. Fangio came in ahead of his team-mate, Luigi Fagioli, the pair three laps clear of the rest of the field. Fangio won again the following year before the race moved.

Reims, too, was not without disasters: Luigi Musso was killed on the sweeping bend that replaced the loop round the village of Gueux.

**ROUEN:** The new French home of Grand Prix lay in a wooded valley of Les-Essarts, south of Rouen in Normandy. The 5.1km (3.2-mile) circuit used the roads winding downhill to Nouveau Monde, a cobbled hairpin and a favourite viewing place.

Initially there was a single race at Rouen in 1952, won by Ascari in a Ferrari, before the focus switched back to Reims for three further races (there was no French Grand Prix in 1955). The circuit was extended to 6.5km (4 miles) in 1955, ready for a return to the action in 1957, when Fangio claimed a masterful victory. From then on the track hosted four more Grands Prix, including the sixth round of the 1968 world championship. Sadly, the 1968 race is best remembered for the fiery crash on its daunting downhill section that claimed the life of Jo Schlesser in his Formula One debut for Honda. As a result of the accident Rouen was removed from the Grand Prix circuit. Today it is cut in half by a new motorway and no longer in use.

**CLERMONT-FERRAND:** Renamed as the Charade circuit, but also known as the Louis Rosier circuit, Clermont-Ferrand was the next French track on the calendar. This 8km (5-mile) mini-Nürburgring, situated in the hills of the Auvergne, had been planned for many years and was eventually built around volcanic plugs in this mountainous region.

# NEVERS MAGNY-COURS

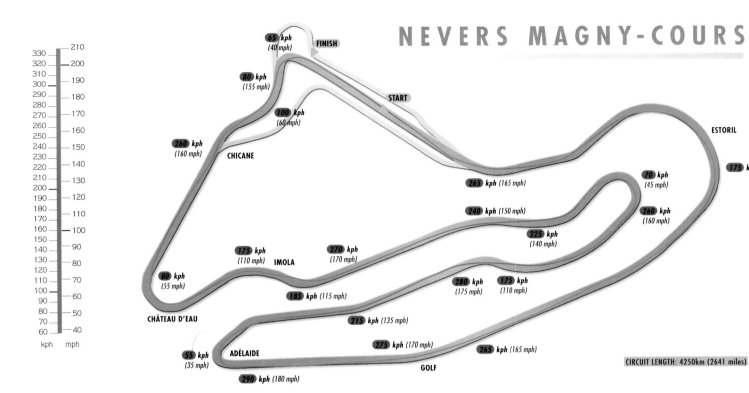

330 — 210
320 — 200
310
300 — 190
290 — 180
280
270 — 170
260 — 160
250
240 — 150
230
220 — 140
210 — 130
200 — 120
190
180 — 110
170
160 — 100
150
140 — 90
130 — 80
120
110 — 70
100 — 60
90
80 — 50
70
60 — 40
kph    mph

**65** *kph (40 mph)* FINISH

**80** *kph (155 mph)*

**100** *kph (60 mph)*

START

**260** *kph (160 mph)* CHICANE

ESTORIL

**175** *kph (110 mph)*

**265** *kph (165 mph)*

**70** *kph (45 mph)*

**240** *kph (150 mph)*

**260** *kph (160 mph)*

**225** *kph (140 mph)*

**175** *kph (110 mph)* IMOLA

**270** *kph (170 mph)*

**80** *kph (55 mph)*

**280** *kph (175 mph)*

**175** *kph (110 mph)*

**185** *kph (115 mph)*

CHÂTEAU D'EAU

**215** *kph (135 mph)*

**275** *kph (170 mph)*

**265** *kph (165 mph)*

**55** *kph (35 mph)* ADÉLAIDE

GOLF

CIRCUIT LENGTH: 4250km (2641 miles)

**290** *kph (180 mph)*

It was developed on public roads and became notorious for its undulating terrain. The debut race in 1965 was won by Jim Clark in a Lotus and four years later, when it next attracted the Grand Prix, his countryman Jackie Stewart took the chequered flag. Clermont-Ferrand hosted two more races before retreating from international events in 1988. The 1970 Grand Prix was won by Jochen Rindt in a Lotus, and in 1972 Jackie Stewart won again, this time in a Tyrrell.

**LE MANS:** There has been motor racing around Le Mans ever since the first Grand Prix was held there in 1906, and the famous Sarthe circuit has been used for the Le Mans 24-Hour Race since 1923.

The Le Mans Bugatti track hosted the French Grand Prix in 1967, the 4.4km (2.75-mile) Bugatti section incorporating part of the Le Mans start-finish straight before turning infield and weaving through the car park. The twisting circuit was unpopular with drivers and

*Top: Magny-Cours is the home of the French Grand Prix.*
*Left: The French showed their enthusiasm for Formula One racing in style at the 1997 Grand Prix; a fly-over left the sky above Magny-Cours streaked in the characteristic red, white and blue of the Tricolor.*

spectators, however, and was used only once for a world championship race that was won by Jack Brabham in his own car.

**PAUL RICARD:** The Paul Ricard track was built in 1969 and hosted its first race two years later. Inspired and financed by drinks magnate Paul Ricard, this modern complex has had a variety of circuit layouts. It was built on a windy plateau at La Castellet, inland of Bandol on the French Riviera.

After the demise of the Dijon-Prenois circuit as a major racing venue, Paul Ricard hosted six races between 1985 and 1990. Two Formula One greats dominated that period: Mansell won in 1986 and 1987, and Prost won three races in a row from 1988.

The track was dominated by the 1.6km (1-mile) Mistral straight that led into the flat-out Signes right-hander. Though there were many accidents here, few resulted in serious injuries – until Elio de Angelis was killed in a testing accident in 1986. After this, the track was shortened to 2.6km (2.4 miles), cutting the length of the Mistral straight by half. Although the track has hosted 14 Grands Prix, its high-speed layout is not conducive to close, wheel-to-wheel racing. Consequently, it is no longer a feature on the Grand Prix calendar.

**DIJON-PRENOIS:** Another circuit came onto the scene at about the same time as the Paul Ricard. This was Dijon-Prenois, situated deep in the Burgundy region. The track built in 1970, measuring just over 3.2km (2 miles), was too short and caused congestion. Even after the addition of the Parabolique loop in 1976 that stretched its length to 3.9km (2.4 miles), it was still not considered long enough.

Nevertheless, Dijon-Prenois proved popular with spectators and hosted four races over a 10-year period, including several memorable ones such as the 1977 race-long battle between Mario Andretti's Lotus and John Watson's Brabham – finally settled in the American's favour only on the final lap.

In 1979 Dijon was the scene of the first Grand Prix victory for a turbo car, with Jean-Pierre Jabouille's win in the Renault Turbo. Despite that historic landmark, the spectators were far more captivated by the dramatic battle for second place between René Arnoux and Gilles Villeneuve, which provided one of the greatest fights in racing history. Yet another important event was the 1981 debut victory of a certain Frenchman who would go on to become his country's most famous racing driver, Alain Prost.

**NEVERS MAGNY-COURS:** Enter the 1990s, and a new hi-tech circuit gained the exclusive rights to the French Grand Prix with assistance from the French premier. Nevers Magny-Cours was redeveloped to feature one of the flattest, smoothest surfaces in motor racing. The home of the Knight brothers' Winfield Racing School and Ligier, Prost, too, has made it its base and moved its factory to the circuit.

Its compact layout makes for excellent viewing, but it is hampered by poor access. There are only two minor roads, from the north and south respectively, and insufficient accommodation to meet the requirements of teams and sponsors.

There is no doubt that Michael Schumacher has mastered Magny-Cours better than any other driver. He has taken the chequered flag on four occasions in a five-year spell, twice in a Benetton (1994 and 1995) and twice in a Ferrari in (1997 and 1998).

Fuchsröhre

Aremberg

Schwedenkreuz

Flugplatz

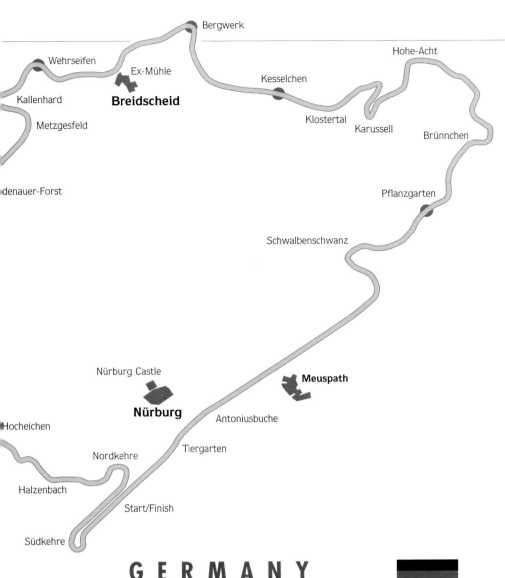

Bergwerk

Wehrseifen

Ex-Mühle

Hohe-Acht

Kesselchen

Kallenhard

**Breidscheid**

Klostertal

Karussell

Brünnchen

Metzgesfeld

Pflanzgarten

denauer-Forst

Schwalbenschwanz

Nürburg Castle

**Meuspath**

**Nürburg**

Antoniusbuche

Hocheichen

Tiergarten

Nordkehre

Halzenbach

Start/Finish

Südkehre

# GERMANY

Germany's stature in Formula One has turned full circle. In racing's fledgling years, the mighty Mercedes team was one of the country's leading lights. Over time, Germany's influence on the track waned, until the 1990s, when a certain Michael Schumacher galvanized German interest, soon followed by Heinz-Harald Frentzen and Ralf Schumacher. The emergence of these drivers coincided with the re-entry of Mercedes into the sport, this time not as a team, but as engine supplier to the mighty McLaren team.

One facet of German racing that never waned was the tracks. The mighty Nürburgring was one of Formula One's greatest challenges. Its replacement, Hockenheim, still holds its place on the 21st-century Formula One schedule.

**NÜRBURGRING:** Probably the greatest racetrack in the world achieved its greatest international attention at a terrible and tragic cost. The 22.8km (14.2-mile) Nürburgring has claimed the lives of five Formula One drivers at Grand Prix meetings alone, leaving many others permanently injured.

Despite its fearsome reputation and appalling safety record, however, the 'Ring hosted 21 Grands Prix between 1951 and 1976. It was a track both loved and feared by the world's best drivers. In the words of Jackie Stewart, 'When I left home before the German Grand Prix, I always used to pause at the end of the driveway and take a long look back. I was never sure I'd come home again.'

The giant track was built as a government employment programme around the village of Nürburg, in the Eifel mountains southwest of Bonn. Officially, it consisted of 176 corners on the 22.8km (14.2-mile) Nordschleife and shorter, separate 7.7km (4.8-mile) Südschleife, and presented a supreme challenge for man and machine.

Hidden deep in the forest-clad mountains lie corners with names like Flugplatz, Aremberg, Bergwerk, Karussell and Pflanzgarten that evoke the memories of old masters. But the Nürburgring spelled

*Above:* **Nürburg castle sits high on a hill overlooking both the old and new Nürburgring circuits.**
*Left:* **Rolf Stommelen drives the Lotus Ford 59B to eighth place in the 1969 German Grand Prix at the old Nürburgring.**

BIT-KURVE

**265** *kph (165 mph)*

**170** *kph (105 mph)*

**290** *kph (120 mph)*

VEEDOL-SCHIKANE

**150** *kph (95 mph)*

RTL-KURVE

**170** *kph (105 mph)*

COCA-COLA KURVE

CASTROL-S

**130** *kph (80 mph)*

**110** *kph (70 mph)*

**255** *kph (160 mph)*

**270** *kph (170 mph)*

**295** *kph (185 mph)*

START/FINISH

**250** *kph (155 mph)*

**175** *kph (110 mph)*

DUNLOP KEHRE

**80** *kph (50 mph)*

FORDKURVE

CIRCUIT LENGTH: 4556km (2831 miles)

**280** *kph (175 mph)*

**105** *kph (65 mph)*

disaster for more Formula One drivers than any other track and faded from international racing on safety grounds. Onofre Marimon was killed at the Wehrseifen Bridge and Peter Collins at Pflanzgarten. Finally, Niki Lauda's near-fatal accident at Bergwerk heralded the end of the circuit as a Grand Prix venue.

The German Grand Prix was absent from the inaugural championship, but when it arrived on the scene in 1951, Alberto Ascari and Ferrari triumphed. The Italian was to repeat this feat the next year and Giuseppe Farina made it three in a row for Ferrari in 1953. The 1954 race, first in a trio of back-to-back victories for Fangio, was marred by the death of Marimon. The third of Fangio's triumphs, in which he chased and passed the Ferraris of Peter Collins and Mike Hawthorn to claim the world championship, was considered by many experts to have been the greatest Formula One performance ever.

Indeed, some drivers seemed to have an affinity with the 'Ring. John Surtees finished first in 1963 and 1964, while Jackie Stewart won there three times (1968, 1971 and 1973). The first win for the Scot was achieved after a magnificent performance in wet conditions.

But growing concerns for the safety of drivers called the 'Ring's suitability for Formula One races into question. It needed just one more incident to tip the scales, and when Niki Lauda nearly perished in his flaming Ferrari in 1976, it was the end of the Nürburgring as a Formula One track.

In recent years motor racing – and even Formula One – has returned to the Nürburgring. But it was not the fearsome old circuit, rather a new, efficient 4.5km (2.8 mile) track nestled in the shadow of its grim elder brother. It held its first Grand Prix, the European Grand Prix, in 1984, won by Alain Prost. It then hosted the German Grand Prix in 1985. Formula One went south again to Hockenheim after that but returned in 1995, first as the European Grand Prix and, latterly, as the Luxembourg Grand Prix.

During the reign of the 'Ring there had been another shortlived pretender to the crown, a pale shadow of the great track. The Automobil Verkehrs- und Übungsstraße (AVUS) was constructed on a dual carriageway in the Grunewald area of Berlin. The unimaginative layout comprised a blast up one side of the dual carriageway, with a loop to return racers back the other way. Even the addition of a 43-degree banking in 1937, though it led to faster times, did nothing to improve the track. The circuit had to be shortened with a new south curve in 1954, as the original section lay in the Soviet sector of Berlin.

*Top left:* **The new Nürburgring, close to Michael Schumacher's birthplace, is always packed with his supporters.**
*Right:* **Action from the 1965 German Grand Prix with Jackie Stewart, in the BRM, rounding one of the old Nürburgring's sweeping bends.**

Jean Behra perished on the banking during the single Grand Prix to be held at AVUS in 1959, a race won by Tony Brooks in a Ferrari. The banking was demolished in 1967 and, after a period of disuse, a shorter circuit was set up for domestic racing.

**HOCKENHEIM:** The demise of the Nürburgring created the need for a new national German racing circuit. That honour went to Hockenheim in the Rhine valley, just south of the university city of Heidelberg.

The Hockenheimring, a 7.7km (4.8-mile) race and test track, had opened in 1932. It became an oval, the Kurpfalzring, six years later and was renamed Hockenheimring shortly after the end of World War II. Then it fell into disuse when the original oval was cut into two by a dual carriageway, but reopened in 1966 with the addition of a stadium section to seat 100,000 spectators.

Hockenheim hosted its first world championship race in 1970 (won by Jochen Rindt in a Lotus). Since 1977, with the exception of 1985, it has been the permanent home of the German Grand Prix. Hockenheim is a strange circuit. In fact, it appears to be two distinct tracks joined together. First there is the fast blast through the forest, which is invisible to spectators massed around the stadium section, followed by two long, sweeping, high-speed straights each with a chicane linked by the Ostkurve. And then there is the stadium section itself, which is slow and tricky. In comparison with the rigours of the Nürburging, the Hockenheim circuit was considered fast, very fast, but yet comparatively safe and rather soulless.

However, even before Formula One first visited the track, it had claimed the life of legendary racer Jim Clark, who died in the Hockenheim forest in a low-priority Formula Two race in 1968. A simple stone cross marks the spot where he perished.

After the initial visit in 1970, Formula One action returned to the Nürburgring for six years, while Hockenheim reverted to hosting Formula Two races. Then Niki Lauda's accident in 1976 sealed the end of the Nürburgring and a new venue had to be sought. Amazingly, Lauda had made a full recovery in time for the 1977 race and, to the delight of local fans, secured a victory at Hockenheim.

The fast forest track claimed another victim in the run-up to the 1980 race, when Patrick Depailler tragically died at the Ostkurve while testing an Alfa Romeo. His countryman, Jacques Laffite, subsequently won a very subdued event. Tragedy struck again in 1982, shortly after the death of Gilles Villeneuve at Zolder, when his estranged

# HOCKENHEIM

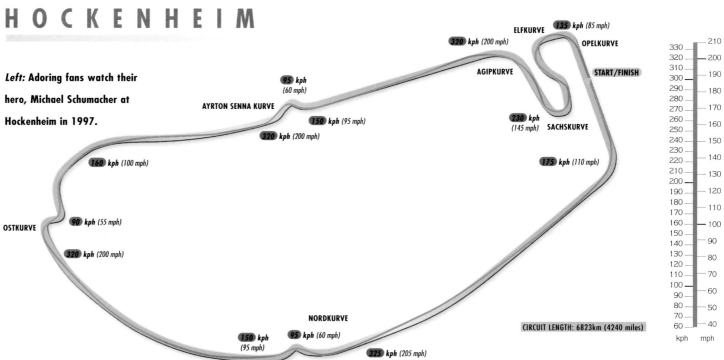

**Left:** Adoring fans watch their hero, Michael Schumacher at Hockenheim in 1997.

ELFKURVE **135** kph *(85 mph)*
**320** kph *(200 mph)* OPELKURVE
AGIPKURVE START/FINISH
AYRTON SENNA KURVE
**95** kph *(60 mph)*
**150** kph *(95 mph)*
**230** kph *(145 mph)* SACHSKURVE
**320** kph *(200 mph)*
**160** kph *(100 mph)* **175** kph *(110 mph)*
OSTKURVE
**90** kph *(55 mph)*
**320** kph *(200 mph)*
NORDKURVE
**150** kph *(95 mph)* **95** kph *(60 mph)*
**325** kph *(205 mph)*

CIRCUIT LENGTH: 6823km (4240 miles)

team-mate, Didier Pironi, had his career cut short after a collision in wet conditions during the qualifying laps. There was a glimmer of hope for the Italian marque when Patrick Tambay scored a memorable victory in the race the following day.

French drivers fared well in the next two years. René Arnoux won for Ferrari in 1983 and Alain Prost in the McLaren the following year. Hockenheim was not lucky for Prost, however, and he could not secure a second victory at the German track until 1993, driving a Williams in his final year in Formula One.

**Top left and above:** The Hockenheim racetrack in southern Germany is the permanent home of the German Grand Prix.

**Below:** The grandstands of Hockenheim's stadium section, awash with German flags, create a marvellous atmosphere for the German Grand Prix.

It was glory for Ferrari again in 1985, when Michele Alboreto scored his fifth and final Formula One victory before the boys from Brazil took over. From 1986 to 1990, a Brazilian claimed victory: Nelson Piquet scored a double in 1986 and 1987 before Ayrton Senna took off with three consecutive wins in his McLaren. It was not until 1995 that a German finally managed to win his home Grand Prix. Not surprisingly, this honour went to the man of the Nineties, none other than Michael Schumacher.

*Below:* **The two Williams Renaults lead the field into the Parabolica, Monza's 180-degree final corner. The *tifosi*, Italy's passionate motor racing fans, line the racetrack.**

# ITALY

There can be no doubt that of all the motor racing fans in the world none come close in terms of passion to the avid *tifosi*, who turn Monza and Imola into virtual shrines to Ferrari each year. Drive for Ferrari and you are a hero, but turn up for the opposition and you'll get an icy reception.

**MONZA:** Apart from having the world's most passionate (not to mention partisan) Formula One fans, Italy has two classic racing venues. Monza hosts the Italian Grand Prix, and Imola is home to the

# MONZA

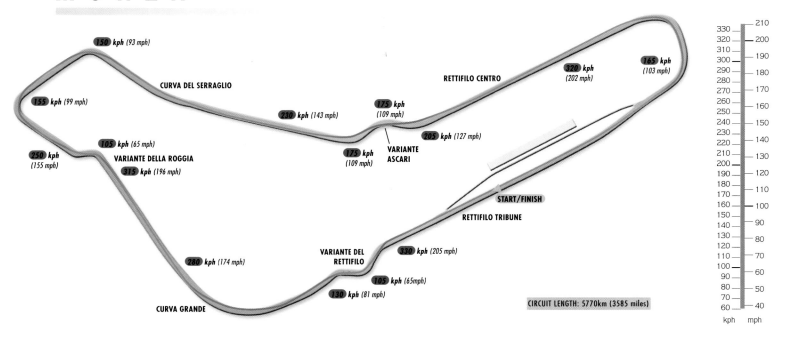

**150 kph** *(93 mph)*

CURVA DEL SERRAGLIO

**155 kph** *(99 mph)*

**230 kph** *(143 mph)*

**175 kph** *(109 mph)*

RETTIFILO CENTRO

**320 kph** *(202 mph)*

**165 kph** *(103 mph)*

**105 kph** *(65 mph)*

**250 kph** *(155 mph)*

VARIANTE DELLA ROGGIA

**315 kph** *(196 mph)*

**175 kph** *(109 mph)*

VARIANTE ASCARI

**205 kph** *(127 mph)*

START/FINISH

RETTIFILO TRIBUNE

VARIANTE DEL RETTIFILO

**330 kph** *(205 mph)*

**280 kph** *(174 mph)*

**105 kph** *(65mph)*

**130 kph** *(81 mph)*

CURVA GRANDE

CIRCUIT LENGTH: 5770km (3585 miles)

San Marino. No motor racing track in Formula One evokes more memories of the sport's golden age than Monza. A quick stroll into the forest, away from the bustle, noise and mayhem of the pits on Grand Prix weekend, brings you to the fearsome banking of the old Monza circuit where you can almost see and hear the ghostly cars of legendary drivers who raced (and died) on this track in its heyday.

The Autodromo Nationale at Monza, to give it its full name, is built in the verdant grounds of the Monza Royal Palace north of Milan. On a clear day, the southern Alps make a stunning backdrop to the palace and the royal park in which the track is set. The first stones of the 10km (6.2-mile) track were laid in February 1922, but work was temporarily halted by environmentalists protesting against the destruction of the forest. It eventually resumed in May, and by the end of August 1922 the shrine was open to the motor racing faithful.

The swift but menacing circuit ceased to host races in 1933 and fell into disrepair, even being used as a military dump during World War II. After the war the road circuit was redeveloped, and in 1955 a banked speedway section, half sunk into the ground, was built. That

banking was used until 1968 and today crumbling sections of the original track can be seen running round the back of the Parabolica.

Monza has the distinction of hosting the fastest and closest Grand Prix ever run. In 1971 Peter Gethin crossed the line just one hundredth of a second ahead of Ronnie Peterson, to win at an amazing average speed of just over 240kph (150mph), ultra high speeds that heralded the introduction of chicanes for the following year.

Not all the memories of Monza are happy ones, however. Over the years, the track has exacted a terrible toll. In 1928 Emilio Materassi perished along with 27 spectators. In 1933, Luigi Arcangeli died, and later that year three spectators were killed when Philippe Etancelin crashed at Lesmo. On one calamitous day of the same year, Giuseppe Campari, Baconin Borzacchini and Count Stanislas Craykowski died. This triple tragedy signalled the end of the original track, but even when racing returned, the toll continued to mount.

Some 12 world championships have been decided in the royal park, including the first when Giuseppe Farina clinched the championship – careering to victory in his Alfa Romeo. The next decider at this hallowed venue came five years later, in the aftermath of the catastrophe

triumph for the Ford Cosworth V8. Other multiple winners were Jackie Stewart and Niki Lauda, both winning the race three times.

Like all tracks Zandvoort had its fair share of racing disasters. Piers Courage lost his life in 1970, and three years later there was the horrific accident that claimed Roger Williamson. The sight of David Purley trying to rescue Williamson from his flaming wreck, while fire marshals hung back in fear, is still a haunting memory.

**ANDERSTORP (SWEDEN):** Another country making a brief appearance on the Formula One calendar in the 1970s was Sweden. Anderstorp was conceived by Sven Asberg and built on flat marshland forest. A runway formed part of the back straight, also known as the Scandinavian Raceway. Throughout its six Grands Prix, the 3.2km (2.5-mile) track was renowned for unpredictable results.

When Formula One first came to Anderstorp in 1973, local legend Ronnie Peterson had yet to win a race for Lotus. He very nearly did so at Anderstorp, but a puncture late in the race allowed Denny Hulme to sweep by to victory. A year later Jody Scheckter earned his debut Formula One victory at Anderstorp, winning a second Swedish Grand Prix in 1976.

Another double Swedish Grand Prix winner was Niki Lauda, who conquered the track in a Ferrari in 1975. He repeated the feat three years later aboard the infamous Brabham fan car that was later banned. The only other man to win a Grand Prix in Sweden was Jacques Laffite, who won the 1977 race for Ligier.

Just a few months after the 1978 race both of the local heroes, Ronnie Peterson and Gunnar Nilsson, were dead (the latter after a tough battle with cancer). The Swedish race perished with them.

*Opposite top:* **Jackie Stewart driving a BRM during the Dutch Grand Prix held at Zandvoort in 1965.**
*Left:* **Riccardo Patrese, driving an Arrows (Number 35), is pursued by a sleek black-and-gold JPS Lotus during the 1978 Swedish Grand Prix at Anderstorp. Niki Lauda, in a Brabham, went on to win.**
*Top right:* **Jochen Rindt, driving the Lotus 72 in its debut race, leads John Surtees during the 1970 Spanish Grand Prix at Járama.**

# SPAIN AND PORTUGAL

Grand Prix racing in Spain dates back to 1913 to an event at Guadarrama, northwest of Madrid. The first race inside the confines of the world championship, however, took place in 1951 at Pedralbes, Barcelona. Over the years Formula One in Spain and its Iberian neighbour, Portugal, has been sporadic at best.

**PEDRALBES (SPAIN):** The Pedralbes track, located 6.4km (3.97 miles) northwest of the Barcelona city centre, incorporated the wide avenues found on the outskirts of the city, in the shadow of the Pedralbes Monastery. A major motor racing venue after World War II, it hosted the famous Penya Rhin pre-world championship event. Fangio won the inaugural Grand Prix in an Alfa Romeo, and when Formula One returned three years later, Mike Hawthorn took the chequered flag in a Ferrari. Soon afterwards the Pedralbes circuit faded from the international calendar.

**JÁRAMA AND MONTJUICH (SPAIN):** Formula One left Spain for 14 years and when it returned Spain's two biggest cities were vying for the honour of hosting the race: Járama in Madrid, and Montjuich Park in Barcelona. Eventually a compromise was reached and for eight years the two circuits shared the race in alternate years.

Járama, located 29km (18 miles) from the Spanish capital, Madrid, was designed by John Hugeholtz to fit into a small pocket of land in the arid, hilly scrublands north of the city. Considered by many to be too cramped for car racing, the circuit is now being used as a motor-cycle race circuit. A golf centre has also developed. Járama's Formula One debut was in 1967 and the 3.4km (2.1-mile) track hosted nine Grands Prix until Formula One left for good after 1981.

**MONTJUICH PARK (SPAIN):** Montjuich Park was situated on undulating roads in a public park overlooking the city centre near Barcelona's Olympic stadium. The circuit was first used in 1933 and was revived in 1966, with a Formula Two race won by Jack Brabham. In 1969 Jackie Stewart won the first Grand Prix at Montjuich, driving a Matra in his championship season, but the race is remembered for two big Lotus crashes: first Graham Hill and, moments later, Jochen Rindt with wing failures caused by the harsh bumps on the park cir-cuit. Jackie Stewart earned his third successive Spanish success when the race returned to Barcelona in 1971, having won at Járama in

1970. Two years later Emerson Fittipaldi of Lotus claimed victory.

The teams were back in 1975 for another of those afternoons that darken the sport's reputation. There had been little practice as the drivers complained about the lack of safety considerations, in partic-ular, bolts missing from the Armco. Reigning world champion, Emerson Fittipaldi, packed his bags and departed on the morning of the race under threat from the Spanish authorities that the cars would be impounded if the race did not take place. Eventually, despite protest, the race began. Several drivers retired early on and there was chaos on the track when car after car crashed out with broken suspensions or drive shafts. Ralf Stommelen was leading after 25 laps before he shed his rear aerofoil and crashed, killing four bystanders. The race was stopped and Jochen Mass was awarded half points. Montjuich Park was finished as a Formula One venue.

**JERÉZ DE LA FRONTERA (SPAIN):** Jeréz reintroduced Formula One to Spain in 1986 after a four-year absence. However, due to its location deep in the sherry producing region of Spain's southern

# JERÉZ

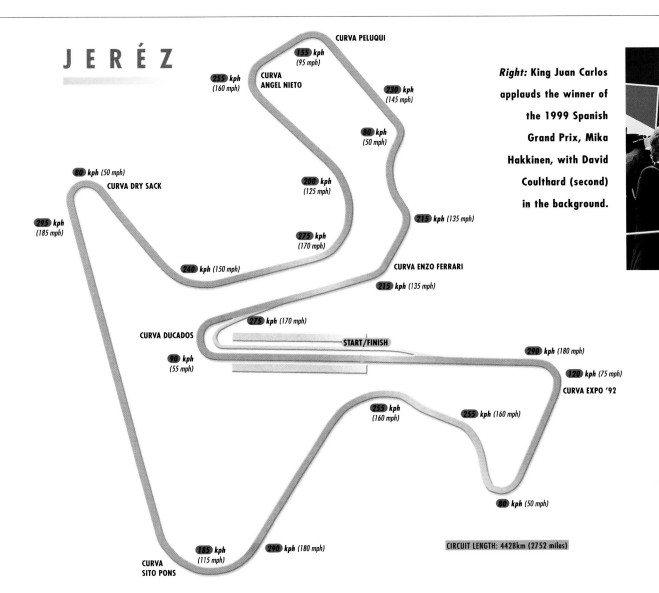

**CURVA PELUQUI**

155 *kph* (95 mph)

255 *kph* (160 mph)

**CURVA ANGEL NIETO**

230 *kph* (145 mph)

80 *kph* (50 mph)

80 *kph* (50 mph)

**CURVA DRY SACK**

200 *kph* (125 mph)

295 *kph* (185 mph)

215 *kph* (135 mph)

275 *kph* (170 mph)

240 *kph* (150 mph)

**CURVA ENZO FERRARI**

215 *kph* (135 mph)

275 *kph* (170 mph)

**CURVA DUCADOS**

**START/FINISH**

290 *kph* (180 mph)

90 *kph* (55 mph)

120 *kph* (75 mph)

**CURVA EXPO '92**

255 *kph* (160 mph)

255 *kph* (160 mph)

80 *kph* (50 mph)

185 *kph* (115 mph)

290 *kph* (180 mph)

**CURVA SITO PONS**

CIRCUIT LENGTH: 4428km (2752 miles)

*Right:* **King Juan Carlos applauds the winner of the 1999 Spanish Grand Prix, Mika Hakkinen, with David Coulthard (second) in the background.**

plains, and the local preference for bike racing, it has never attracted large Formula One crowds. It was dropped from the calendar after Martin Donnelly's accident during a practice session in 1990, which left the broken and twisted Ulsterman lying on the track, still strapped to his seat – the force of the collision with the concrete barrier had shattered the car around him. Donnelly recovered from

*Above:* **Jeréz in southern Spain has hosted the Spanish Grand Prix and, more recently, two European Grands Prix.**
*Left:* **The starting grid of the Spanish Grand Prix at Jeréz, a permanent road course first opened in 1986.**

his injuries, but his Formula One career was over. Grand Prix racing returned briefly with two European Grands Prix, after a chicane had been added before the corner where Donnelly had his accident.

**CIRCUIT DE CATALUNYA (SPAIN):** It was left to Barcelona to mount a challenge for a place in the Grand Prix calender. This it did by producing the Montemelo circuit, built 19.3km (12 miles) north of Barcelona on land purchased by the Royal Automovil Club de Catalunya, with the aim of bringing Formula One back to the spiritual home of Spanish motorsport. It was the third Formula One track to be used in Barcelona and was completed just in time for the 1991 Grand Prix. In fact, the paint was still wet when the teams arrived.

# ESTORIL

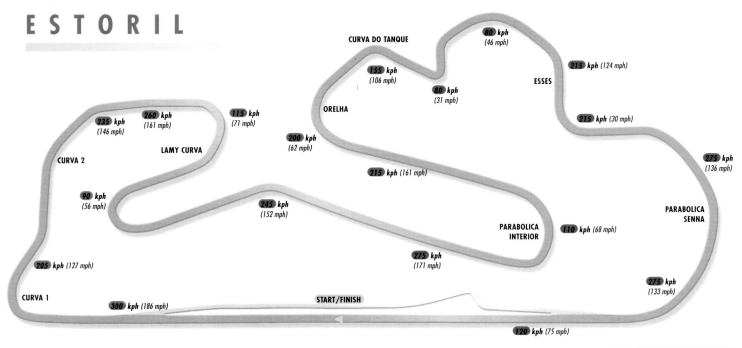

CURVA DO TANQUE

80 kph (46 mph)

155 kph (106 mph)

80 kph (31 mph)

ORELHA

ESSES

215 kph (124 mph)

215 kph (30 mph)

235 kph (146 mph)

260 kph (161 mph)

115 kph (71 mph)

200 kph (62 mph)

LAMY CURVA

CURVA 2

90 kph (56 mph)

245 kph (152 mph)

215 kph (161 mph)

275 kph (136 mph)

PARABOLICA INTERIOR

110 kph (68 mph)

PARABOLICA SENNA

205 kph (127 mph)

275 kph (171 mph)

275 kph (133 mph)

CURVA 1

300 kph (186 mph)

START/FINISH

120 kph (75 mph)

CIRCUIT LENGTH: 4.359km (2.709 miles)

The facilities are excellent at Montemelo. The track is well laid out and incorporates good viewing positions for the spectators. Luis Perez Sala, a retired Spanish Formula One driver, advised on the 4,7km (2.9-mile) circuit, which – although it features one of the longest main straights in today's Formula One – follows the basic principles of most modern-day circuits.

Nigel Mansell took an instant liking to the track, claiming back-to-back victories in the first two races in his Williams Renault. In fact, it seemed as though Williams were suited to the fast, sweeping layout, when Prost and Hill took the honours in the next two races, both driving Williams Renault machines.

The sequence was broken by Michael Schumacher with two victories, first for Benetton and the following year aboard a Ferrari. The first race of the new millennium also looked like going the way of Michael Schumacher, before a calamitous pitstop during which he ran over his chief mechanic, Nigel Stepney. Victory went to Mika Hakkinen in the McLaren Mercedes.

**PORTO (PORTUGAL):** Spain's neighbour, Portugal, has also had several venues host a round of the world championship. The first was the northern coastal town of Porto. The circuit at Porto was a true street

circuit, situated close to the harbour front and incorporating part of a dual carriageway. Its layout included all manner of hazards with houses, shops, lamp posts, cobbles and even tram lines to contend with. It was used for sports car racing, but hosted two Grands Prix in 1958 and 1960, which were won by Stirling Moss in the Vanwall and Jack Brabham in the Cooper Climax, respectively. It was generally considered dangerous and was not used after 1960.

**MONSANTO PARK (PORTUGAL):** Next was Monsanto Park in Lisbon, a natural circuit, built in 1954 around the roads of a picturesque park. Its main straight was a section of the dual carriageway that formed part of the road from Lisbon to Estoril. The circuit, too, was used for sports car racing, but hosted one Grand Prix in 1959 (won by Stirling Moss). After that it faded from the international scene.

*Above:* Estoril circuit near Portugal's capital city, Lisbon, hosted a total of 13 Portuguese Grands Prix in the 1980s and 90s.
*Right:* The long run to the first corner at Estoril is always a highlight of the Portuguese Grand Prix.

**ESTORIL (PORTUGAL):** Nowadays, when Formula One and Portugal are mentioned together, most people think of Estoril. Situated some 24km (15 miles) along the coast west of Lisbon, the Estoril track is built on a barren, rocky plateau, inland of the popular beach resort. It was built in 1972 and was used for local races in its early years before falling into disrepair. Redeveloped for international racing in the early 1980s, it hosted the first of its 13 Grands Prix in 1984. That race not only marked Formula One's return to Portugal after a 24-year absence, it was also the title decider. Alain Prost claimed victory in the McLaren, his team-mate Niki Lauda coming in second but managing to clinch the championship by half a point.

The race the following year was another landmark, with a talented young Brazilian by the name of Ayrton Senna winning in the wet to claim his first Grand Prix victory. It was ostensibly on the grounds of safety that, in 1996, Estoril ceased to be a Formula One venue. However, many believe the true reason is an ongoing financial dispute with Bernie Ecclestone, the king of Formula One.

The period from 1990 to 1996 was a good one for the Williams Renault team at Estoril. The English outfit won five of the six races at Estoril, with five different drivers: Riccardo Patrese, Nigel Mansell, Damon Hill, David Coulthard and Jacques Villeneuve. The man who spoiled the clean sweep was, not surprisingly, Michael Schumacher who won the 1993 race.

# ÖSTERREICHRING/A1-RING

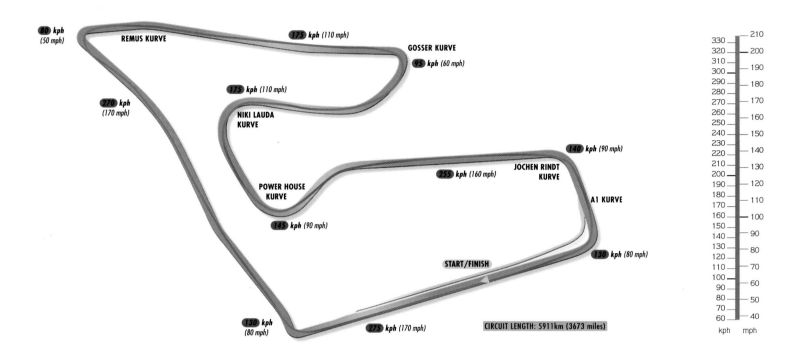

**80 kph** *(50 mph)*
REMUS KURVE
**175 kph** *(110 mph)*
GOSSER KURVE
**95 kph** *(60 mph)*
**175 kph** *(110 mph)*
**270 kph** *(170 mph)*
NIKI LAUDA KURVE
**140 kph** *(90 mph)*
**255 kph** *(160 mph)*
JOCHEN RINDT KURVE
POWER HOUSE KURVE
A1 KURVE
**145 kph** *(90 mph)*
**130 kph** *(80 mph)*
START/FINISH
**130 kph** *(80 mph)*
**275 kph** *(170 mph)*
CIRCUIT LENGTH: 5911km (3673 miles)

| kph | mph |
|---|---|
| 330 | 210 |
| 320 | 200 |
| 310 | 190 |
| 300 | |
| 290 | 180 |
| 280 | |
| 270 | 170 |
| 260 | 160 |
| 250 | |
| 240 | 150 |
| 230 | |
| 220 | 140 |
| 210 | 130 |
| 200 | |
| 190 | 120 |
| 180 | 110 |
| 170 | |
| 160 | 100 |
| 150 | |
| 140 | 90 |
| 130 | 80 |
| 120 | |
| 110 | 70 |
| 100 | |
| 90 | 60 |
| 80 | 50 |
| 70 | |
| 60 | 40 |

# SWITZERLAND, AUSTRIA AND HUNGARY

Three countries in central Europe have, in their own way, added to the history and mystique of Formula One. The first of these is Switzerland, where motor racing has been banned for more than 45 years; the second, Austria, has one of the most beautiful tracks ever to have hosted a Grand Prix, with the unusual hazard of deer crossing the track; the third is Hungary, the first country from behind the former Iron Curtain to host a Grand Prix.

**BREMGARTEN (SWITZERLAND):** Cars first raced at Bremgarten in 1934. The 7.3km (4.5-mile) track wove its way through winding Swiss forest roads, had no straights to speak of and, with trees overhanging the circuit and even incorporating some cobbled streets, it took its toll on both cars and drivers.

Switzerland can lay claim to being part of the inaugural world championship in 1950, when Giuseppe Farina won the fourth world championship Grand Prix in June of that year driving an Alfa, just ahead of his team-mate, Luigi Fagioli. The following year, the Swiss race opened the campaign and, once again, an Alfa came home in front, this one driven by Juan Manuel Fangio.

Interestingly, both winners of the first two Swiss Grands Prix went on to win the world championship in the year of their Swiss triumphs.

Piero Taruffi won in a Ferrari in 1952, and if he was counting on that sequence to continue he was to be disappointed. He was the only winner of the five Swiss Grands Prix that did not go on to win that year's championship. In fact, his victory in 1952 proved to be the Italian's only success in seven years of Formula One.

Motor racing came to an end at Bremgarten, as it did in the rest of Switzerland, when the government banned the sport in the wake of the 1955 Le Mans disaster. The ban still stands, although a Swiss Grand Prix was held across the border in Dijon-Prenois, France, in 1982.

**ÖSTERREICHRING / A1-RING (AUSTRIA):** Switzerland's Alpine neighbour, Austria, had held 22 races before the turn of the millennium. Formula One first arrived in Austria in 1964 at the 3.2km (2-mile) Zeltweg circuit, 6.4km (4 miles) east of Knittelfeld. The L-shaped track, with its uneven surface proved unsuitable and, after most of the front runners fell by the wayside, victory went to the Ferrari of Lorenzo Bandini, his one and only Formula One success.

The Österreichring was built in the Styrian hills above the airfield circuit of Zeltweg. The scenic 5.8km (3.6-mile) track rises and falls in a natural hillside bowl and, until its 1987 fall from Formula One favour, was a favourite with drivers, especially local hero Gerhard Berger.

The first world championship race at the track took place in 1970

*Left:* **Austria's Österreichring was replaced by the shorter A1-Ring in 1997, which today is home of the Austrian Grand Prix.**
*Below:* **Sparks fly as the titanium underside of Nigel Mansell's Williams comes into contact with the bumpy surface of the Österreichring.**

when another Austrian, Jochen Rindt, led the championship. The grandstands erupted when Rindt took pole position, but in the race he was forced to cede to the Ferrari pair of Jacky Ickx and Clay Regazzoni. Just three weeks later Rindt was dead, killed in practice for the Italian Grand Prix. He was crowned world champion posthumously.

Jo Siffert won in 1971, crossing the line just seconds in front of the fast-closing Emerson Fittipaldi. The Brazilian had his turn the following year and in 1973 it was another Lotus man, Ronnie Peterson, who took the chequered flag.

The year 1975 was not a happy one at the Österreichring. American racer Mark Donohue lost his life after an accident in qualifying. Then, in a race marred by appalling weather, Vittorio Brambilla blighted the celebrations for his sole Formula One triumph by crashing while he waved to the crowd. In the aftermath of Donohue's accident, Hella Licht, the fast right-handed first corner just after the brow of a hill, was eased for the 1976 race.

Österreichring was one of those circuits capable of throwing up a

# HUNGARORING

**Left:** David Coulthard in the McLaren Mercedes on his way to second place at the 1999 Hungarian Grand Prix.

130 kph (80 mph)

225 kph (140 mph)

220 kph (140 mph)

160 kph (100 mph)

185 kph (115 mph)

100 kph (60 mph)

240 kph (150 mph)

225 kph (140 mph)

130 kph (80 mph)

265 kph (165 mph)

95 kph (60 mph)

130 kph (80 mph)

000 kph (000 mph)

105 kph (65 mph)

START/FINISH

115 kph (70 mph)

275 kph (170 mph)

**CIRCUIT LENGTH: 3972km (2468 miles)**

| 330 | 210 |
| 320 | 200 |
| 310 | |
| 300 | 190 |
| 290 | 180 |
| 280 | |
| 270 | 170 |
| 260 | 160 |
| 250 | |
| 240 | 150 |
| 230 | |
| 220 | 140 |
| 210 | 130 |
| 200 | |
| 190 | 120 |
| 180 | 110 |
| 170 | |
| 160 | 100 |
| 150 | |
| 140 | 90 |
| 130 | 80 |
| 120 | |
| 110 | 70 |
| 100 | |
| 90 | 60 |
| 80 | 50 |
| 70 | |
| 60 | 40 |
| kph | mph |

surprise, as it did in 1976, when John Watson claimed the only Formula One victory for the American Penske team. The following year it was the turn of the Shadow team to claim their first and last Formula One triumph, with Alan Jones at the wheel. The Australian claimed his second victory two years later, one of only three men to win more than a single race around the sweeping mountain track. Ronnie Peterson was another, his second victory sandwiched between Jones' two wins.

**Above:** Hungary's Hungaroring circuit near Budapest is a narrow track with slow corners and limited overtaking opportunities.
**Right:** The track is a hive of activity as mechanics cluster around their cars in preparation for the 1986 Hungarian Grand Prix, while hundreds of eager fans jostle for position along the fence and on the grandstand.

However, if anyone can be said to have tamed the track it was Alain Prost, who won there in 1983, as well as '85 and '86. The final race held at the old Österreichring fell to Nigel Mansell in the Williams after the event had to be restarted twice following time-consuming startline pile-ups.

Formula One left Austria for 10 years. When it returned in 1997, it was to a new 4.3km (2.7-mile) track built on the famous fast sweeps of the old circuit. Shackled by modern regulations, the new track is but a pale shadow of its former self – little more than a dull series of second- and third-gear corners with no significant straight. But a track with such magnificent vistas may be forgiven some shortcomings, particularly in view of the exciting fare that it has served in its first years back on the calendar. Jacques Villeneuve won in the

Williams Renault on the return to Austria while Mika Hakkinen won in 1998 after a battle with his nemesis, Michael Schumacher.

**HUNGARORING (HUNGARY):** Last of the central European venues is Hungary. When Formula One first visited the Hungaroring 19km (12 miles) northeast of Budapest in 1986, the country was still in the grip of communism. Now, one of the pleasures of visiting this historic European capital is to note the changes wrought by commercialism.

If the 3.8km (2.5-mile) Hungaroring is famous for anything at all, it is the lack of overtaking opportunities, as was demonstrated in 1990, when Thierry Boutsen led a snaking train of cars (including a highly frustrated Ayrton Senna) from green light to chequered flag, to claim his third and final Formula One victory.

With overtaking all but impossible, to qualify well is vital at the Hungaroring and so it was no surprise that in the track's early days, Senna, the ultimate single-lap racer, was most successful. He won three Hungarian Grands Prix in 1988, '91 and '92, while his country-man Nelson Piquet had opened the Hungarian record books with back-to-back victories in his Williams Honda in 1986 and '87.

One of the most memorable victories was Nigel Mansell's in 1989, coming from 13th position on the grid, when he famously slungshot his Ferrari past Senna who had momentarily hesitated while lapping a backmarker. However, such moments are few and far between at this track. Hungaroring has only really come into its own in the late 1990s with the advent of tactical fuel stops, which can be used to gain track position and do away with the need for overtaking.

# SOUTH AFRICA, AUSTRALIA AND THE EAST

## SOUTH AFRICA

Only three racetracks on the vast African continent have had the honour of staging a Formula One world championship race and only one can claim to have been a regular venue.

In the period immediately following World War II, Africa was better known for its international rallies and adventure races, events that included the world renowned Paris-Dakar and the Safari Rally. In North Africa, the influence of Italian and French rule between the wars lingered on, with small pockets of motor racing activity.

As the Formula One world championship began to take root in Europe in the early 1950s, only three tracks of any significance existed on the African continent. All of these were in South Africa: Gunner's Circle in Cape Town, Grand Central in Johannesburg and the Roy Hesketh Circuit in Pietermaritzburg. By the time the decade had drawn to a close, only Hesketh survived, but it was too narrow and bumpy to be considered a suitable venue for Formula One.

*Left:* **Richie Ginther in the BRM leads Lorenzo Bandini in the Ferrari in the 1963 South African Grand Prix at East London.**
*Previous pages:* **Ayrton Senna in the John Player Special Lotus at Adelaide.**

**EAST LONDON:** The picturesque East London circuit, set in a natural parkland bowl, opened for business in 1959. The 4km (2.43-mile) circuit utilized sections of a pre-war track, on a site that had initially hosted Formula Libre races, before securing the first of its three Grand Prix fixtures in 1962.

The Formula One circus came back the following year and then, after a year away from Africa, returned to East London in 1965.

**KYALAMI:** In the meantime, a group of local businessmen had replaced the obsolete Grand Central track with Kyalami. Built on a plateau 1500m (5000ft) above sea level, 24km (15 miles) north of Johannesburg, the circuit was completed in 1961. Its most striking feature was a very fast, very long downhill main straight. Initially, the circuit had to make do with the non-championship Rand Grand Prix, but as the circuit continued to improve, South Africans began to lobby for a championship race. Finally, in 1966 they were granted the prestigious season-opening race of 1967, an honour they held until 1972. After a major upgrade, which included widening and resurfacing various sections of the track, they were ready for their big day.

The circuit has been the scene of some famous races over the years. Kyalami's initial race was won by Pedro Rodriguez in a Cooper-Maserati, ahead of John Love and John Surtees. Carlos

# KYALAMI

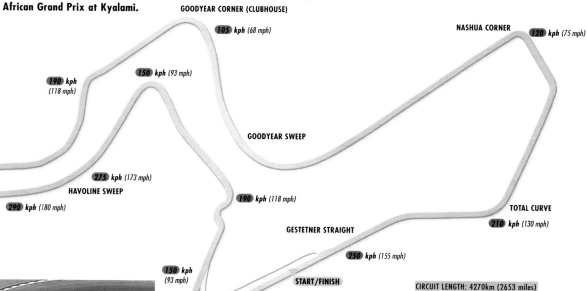

*Left:* **Williams team-mates Nigel Mansell and Riccardo Patrese celebrate after the 1992 South African Grand Prix at Kyalami.**

**GOODYEAR CORNER (CLUBHOUSE)**
**105** *kph* (68 mph)

**NASHUA CORNER**
**120** *kph* (75 mph)

**150** *kph* (93 mph)

**190** *kph*
(118 mph)

**WESBANK CORNER**

**GOODYEAR SWEEP**

**240** *kph* (149 mph)

**275** *kph* (173 mph)

**HAVOLINE SWEEP**

**190** *kph* (118 mph)

**190** *kph*
(118 mph)

**290** *kph* (180 mph)

**TOTAL CURVE**

**210** *kph* (130 mph)

**GESTETNER STRAIGHT**

**150** *kph*
(93 mph)

**250** *kph* (155 mph)

**START/FINISH**

**CIRCUIT LENGTH: 4270km (2653 miles)**

Reutemann secured his first Grand Prix victory in the 1974 race, and two years later the race featured one of the sport's closest finishes with Niki Lauda and James Hunt separated by less than one-and-a-half seconds.

As well as good days, Kyalami holds sad memories. Peter Revson lost his life there in 1974 in a pre-race test. Three years later Tom Pryce died when his Shadow-Ford struck a marshal who was crossing the track.

Permanent facilities at Kyalami were first class and, combined with the excellent winter climate, they made the track Africa's premier venue and a favourite for pre-season testing. High altitude and

*Left:* **Fans pack the grandstands awaiting the start at Kyalami.**
*Top:* **Kyalami returned to the Formula One calendar in 1992 and 1993.**
*Right:* **Nigel Mansell cruises around Kyalami in the Williams FW14B on the way to the first of nine victories in his championship season of 1992.**

associated thin air at the track also made it especially suitable for the turbo engines that dominated motorsport in the early 1980s.

As the 1980s advanced, the political situation in South Africa continued to deteriorate. When several teams boycotted the 1985 race for political reasons, notably the French, it came as no surprise that Kyalami was taken off the Formula One circuit.

Grand Prix action briefly returned to the Kyalami track in 1992 and 1993 and discovered that substantial alterations had been made which left the track characterless and the race slow. Both races were won by Williams-Renaults driven by Nigel Mansell and Alain Prost respectively. Africa has been omitted from the racing calendar since then, although Kyalami is back on the winter testing schedule.

# AUSTRALIA

As far as the Formula One world championship is concerned the Australian continent has only two venues of note. Both of them are street circuits, one in Adelaide, the other in Melbourne.

 The first world championship Australian Grand Prix took place around the streets of Adelaide in 1985. It was the brainchild of Bill O'Gorman, who enlisted the support of John Bannon, South Australia's prime minister. He, in turn, negotiated with Bernie Ecclestone, the driving force behind Formula One. After a series of tough negotiations and a last-minute flight to London, the deal was

struck and Australia had the rights to stage a Grand Prix in Adelaide every year for seven years, starting in 1985. From its inception, this race proved popular with teams and spectators alike, partially due to its position as the final race of a long season, but more importantly because of the festive atmosphere that pervaded the race weekend.

*Above:* **The Simtek Ford in its only appearance, during the 1993 Australian Grand Prix at Adelaide.**
*Inset:* **The high spirits of the local spectators created a party atmosphere at the end-of-season race.**
*Right:* **The grid and pits area at Adelaide; the Victoria Park racecourse, through which the track winds its way, is in the background.**

Adelaide is one of the best street circuits. The wide 3.8km (2.4-mile) track winds its way around the parks of the city and takes in part of the Victoria Park racecourse. The main straight, long for a street circuit, is best remembered for the dramatic tyre blow-out which cost Mansell the world championship in 1986.

The first race round the streets of Adelaide was won with a virtuoso performance by Keke Rosberg in the Williams Honda Turbo. The drama heightened in the following year with Mansell, Prost and Piquet battling for the title. Race victory and the world championship seemed to be in Mansell's hands, until his tyre exploded.

Apart from that incident, Adelaide's most famous and controversial race was the 1994 championship showdown between Damon Hill and Michael Schumacher. Hill in the Williams-Renault came into the race a point behind Schumacher in the Benetton-Ford, after a fractious season-long battle. Williams had drafted Nigel Mansell back to aid Hill's challenge, and the former world champion claimed pole position ahead of Schumacher. On race day, all eyes were on the contenders for the title. The Benetton man had the advantage in the early action, drawing out a significant lead. But Hill clawed back the advantage, putting Schumacher under increasing pressure until the

# MELBOURNE

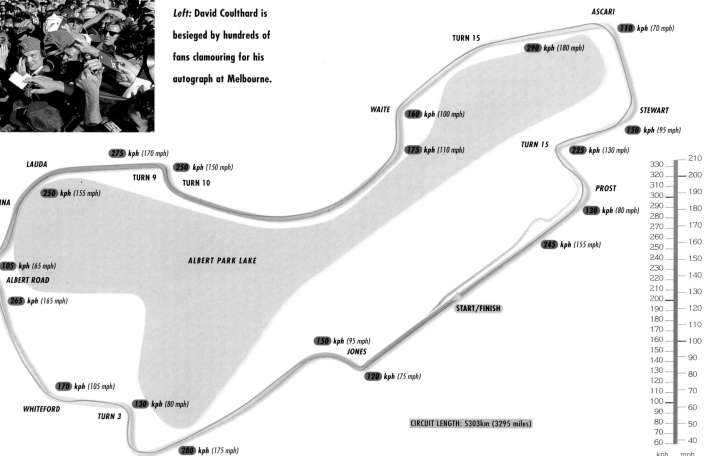

*Left:* David Coulthard is besieged by hundreds of fans clamouring for his autograph at Melbourne.

ASCARI
**110** *kph (70 mph)*

TURN 15
**290** *kph (180 mph)*

WAITE
**160** *kph (100 mph)*

STEWART
**150** *kph (95 mph)*

**175** *kph (110 mph)*

TURN 15
**225** *kph (130 mph)*

**275** *kph (170 mph)*

LAUDA
**250** *kph (150 mph)*

TURN 9
TURN 10

PROST
**130** *kph (80 mph)*

MARINA
**250** *kph (155 mph)*

**245** *kph (155 mph)*

ALBERT PARK LAKE

**105** *kph (65 mph)*
ALBERT ROAD

**265** *kph (165 mph)*

START/FINISH

**150** *kph (95 mph)*
JONES

**120** *kph (75 mph)*

**170** *kph (105 mph)*

WHITEFORD       TURN 3
**130** *kph (80 mph)*

**280** *kph (175 mph)*

**80** *kph (50 mph)*

CIRCUIT LENGTH: 5303km (3295 miles)

| kph | mph |
| --- | --- |
| 330 | 210 |
| 320 | 200 |
| 310 | 190 |
| 300 | |
| 290 | 180 |
| 280 | |
| 270 | 170 |
| 260 | 160 |
| 250 | |
| 240 | 150 |
| 230 | |
| 220 | 140 |
| 210 | 130 |
| 200 | |
| 190 | 120 |
| 180 | 110 |
| 170 | |
| 160 | 100 |
| 150 | |
| 140 | 90 |
| 130 | 80 |
| 120 | |
| 110 | 70 |
| 100 | |
| 90 | 60 |
| 80 | 50 |
| 70 | |
| 60 | 40 |

German driver was forced into an error, glancing the wall. Unbeknown to Hill, this collision would end his challenger's race. Hill then rounded a bend to see a slow-moving car in the middle of the track. He jinked to pass, but Schumacher blocked him with the Benetton, causing a crash that took both men out of the race and earned him the world championship in contentious fashion.

Formula One left Adelaide following the 1995 race and headed for Melbourne to open the campaign of 1996, four months later.

**MELBOURNE:** Melbourne, the state capital of Victoria, is one of the continent's most southerly cities, located across the Bass Straight from Tasmania. Victoria is known as the Garden State, for its tree-lined boulevards and beautiful parks.

The Melbourne Grand Prix circuit was built to run through Albert Park for the Australian Grand Prix race of 1996. Much to the chagrin of the local 'Save Albert Park' campaign and apart from reprofiling, it has remained unchanged since then. The layout of the track is more demanding on the drivers than the average street circuit. The 5.26km (3.3-mile) track is fairly open and doesn't feature any significant straight. A predominance of 75- to 90-degree corners, however, makes set-up, after the teams' pre-season work on fast tracks, a lottery.

*Above:* Melbourne took over the hosting of the Australian Grand Prix in 1996 on a track built around the Albert Park lake. This race opens the Formula One season each year.

Damon Hill had consigned his disagreeable memories of Adelaide to history and scooped a victory in the final Grand Prix held there, in 1995. Then he repeated the feat in the opening race at Melbourne. Millions of TV viewers will remember the 1996 outing for its images of Martin Brundle's dramatic barrel roll on the first start, if not for the sight of him climbing from his ravaged Jordan and sprinting for the pits to take the restart in the spare car.

The next two seasons were dominated by McLaren, David Coulthard getting the 1997 campaign off to a flying start with his first win for McLaren, ending the team's three-year drought. Its previous race victory had been Ayrton Senna's win at the 1993 Australian Grand Prix, his last ever. In 1998 Coulthard looked to be on course again until he controversially slowed to allow team-mate Mika Hakkinen to take the

chequered flag, thus helping the Finnish driver towards his first world championship. To round off the millennium Ferrari scored a double at Melbourne, Eddie Irvine winning the last race of the 20th century and Michael Schumacher the first of the new one.

Whilst the homely charms of Adelaide are still sorely missed by the Formula One fraternity, the bustling, sport-loving city of Melbourne is growing to be a favoured season-opening race.

*Above:* **The controversial collision with Damon Hill at Adelaide that earned Michael Schumacher the 1994 world championship.**
*Below:* **An aerial view of Melbourne's Albert Park track. It is considered to be among the best of Formula One's temporary road courses.**

# S U Z U K A

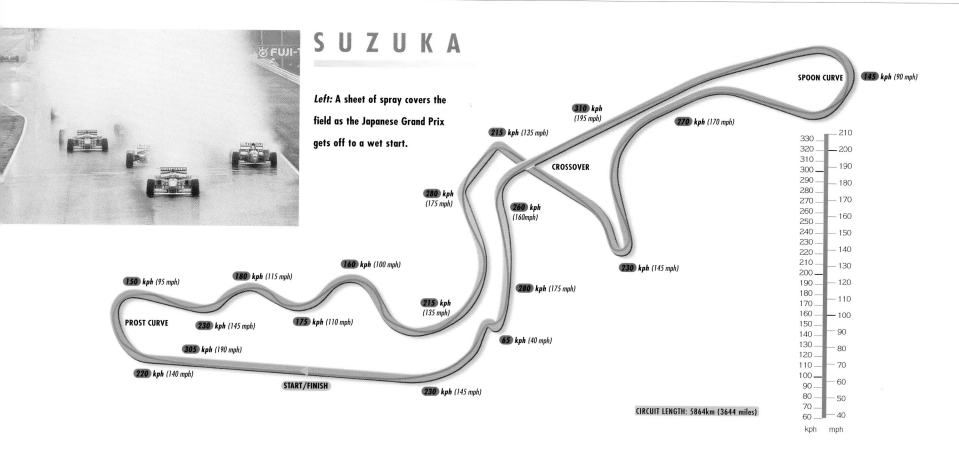

**Left:** A sheet of spray covers the field as the Japanese Grand Prix gets off to a wet start.

SPOON CURVE

**145** kph *(90 mph)*

**310** kph *(195 mph)*

**270** kph *(170 mph)*

**215** kph *(135 mph)*

CROSSOVER

**280** kph *(175 mph)*

**260** kph *(160mph)*

**230** kph *(145 mph)*

**160** kph *(100 mph)*

**180** kph *(115 mph)*

**150** kph *(95 mph)*

**280** kph *(175 mph)*

**215** kph *(135 mph)*

PROST CURVE

**230** kph *(145 mph)*

**175** kph *(110 mph)*

**65** kph *(40 mph)*

**305** kph *(190 mph)*

**220** kph *(140 mph)*

START/FINISH

**230** kph *(145 mph)*

CIRCUIT LENGTH: 5864km (3644 miles)

| kph | mph |
|---|---|
| 330 | 210 |
| 320 | 200 |
| 310 | |
| 300 | 190 |
| 290 | 180 |
| 280 | |
| 270 | 170 |
| 260 | 160 |
| 250 | |
| 240 | 150 |
| 230 | |
| 220 | 140 |
| 210 | 130 |
| 200 | |
| 190 | 120 |
| 180 | |
| 170 | 110 |
| 160 | |
| 150 | 100 |
| 140 | 90 |
| 130 | |
| 120 | 80 |
| 110 | |
| 100 | 70 |
| 90 | 60 |
| 80 | |
| 70 | 50 |
| 60 | 40 |
| kph | mph |

# J A P A N

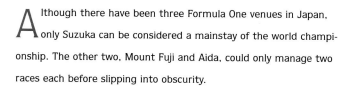

Although there have been three Formula One venues in Japan, only Suzuka can be considered a mainstay of the world championship. The other two, Mount Fuji and Aida, could only manage two races each before slipping into obscurity.

**FUJI INTERNATIONAL SPEEDWAY:** It was the Mount Fuji circuit that first introduced Formula One to Japan with Grands Prix in 1976 and 1977, both dramatic events for different reasons. Fuji International Speedway was originally planned as a giant super speedway, but the plan was eventually scrapped for lack of funds. It lies 64km (40 miles) west of Yokohama in the shadow of the perfectly conical dormant volcano, Mount Fuji. The main feature of the 4.3km (2.67-mile) track was the long front straight and sweeping right-handed corner leading onto it.

The first Formula One action at the track was one of the sport's most dramatic afternoons, the final race of the 1976 campaign.

All eyes were on Niki Lauda, racing just three months after his near-fatal accident at the Nürburgring. He was just three points ahead of Britain's James Hunt in the race for the world championship. Typical of the Mount Fuji region, the day was wet. Very wet. Although the start was delayed to see if conditions would improve, they were still bad by the time the race got under way. Lauda, doubtlessly mindful of his recent brush with death, decided that it was not worth risking his life in pursuit of the world championship and parked his Ferrari in the pits after just three laps.

Hunt needed to earn third place and, after pitting for tyres late in the race, he rejoined in fifth place with four laps to go. Fortunately for him others were also suffering from bad tyre wear – Hunt managed to make it past Clay Regazzoni and Alan Jones to finish third and claim the championship title.

The following year Hunt won the race after a collision between Gilles Villeneuve and Ronnie Peterson sent Villeneuve's car flying into a prohibited area, killing two spectators.

# THE AMERICAS

## CANADA, UNITED STATES, MEXICO, BRAZIL AND ARGENTINA

### CANADA

Canada was a relatively late arrival on the Formula One scene. Its large southern neighbour, the United States, was quicker off the blocks, having hosted a Grand Prix eight years before Canada's 1967 debut at Mosport Park.

**MOSPORT PARK:** The first four Canadian Grands Prix alternated between Mosport Park and Mont Tremblant before Mosport took over, finally losing out to Montreal in 1978.

Mosport Park is located on a wooded hill, on the north bank of Lake Ontario, 97km (60 miles) northeast of Toronto. It opened for racing in 1961. Prior to its Grand Prix debut it hosted the first international motor race in Canada, the Player's 200, which was won by Stirling Moss. The 4km (2.48-mile) circuit with its sweeping

*Left:* **The hairpin at Montreal with the much-photographed pavilion, remnant of the World Trade Fair, in the background.**

*Previous pages:* **An exuberant Ferrari team celebrates Michael Schumacher's victory at the Indianapolis Grand Prix in September 2000.**

bends, is regarded as too dangerous for modern Formula One cars. Manfred Winkelhock was killed in a sports car race and serious accidents befell John Surtees in a Can Am race and Ian Ashley in Grand Prix practice. Apart from the danger, Mosport Park is remembered for its rain. The inaugural Grand Prix in 1967 was dominated by rain and the Repco-Brabham team, Jack Brabham winning ahead of his team-mate, Denny Hulme. Two years later when the race returned to Mosport Park, Brabham again collected top honours courtesy of Jacky Ickx in his Ford-powered car.

Jackie Stewart won in 1971 and '72 in a Tyrrell-Ford, the first time in rain, the second in fog. It rained again the following year, but that did not deter Peter Revson who won his second and last Formula One victory in a McLaren-Ford. In fact, Mosport Park proved to be good for the McLaren team, with Emerson Fittipaldi collecting top honours in 1974 and Hunt winning the next race there in 1976. The track's tenure as Formula One venue ended with a victory for South African Jody Scheckter in a Wolf-Ford in 1977.

**MONT TREMBLANT:** Mont Tremblant (St Jovite) is situated in the scenic woodlands of the Laurentian Mountains, about 145km (90 miles) north of Montreal. The circuit was lengthened to Grand Prix standards in 1966, but was regarded as too narrow and only

# MONTREAL

**Right:** Poor weather conditions forced
the rescheduling of the Montreal event
from the end-of-season berth to its
now traditional mid-season position.

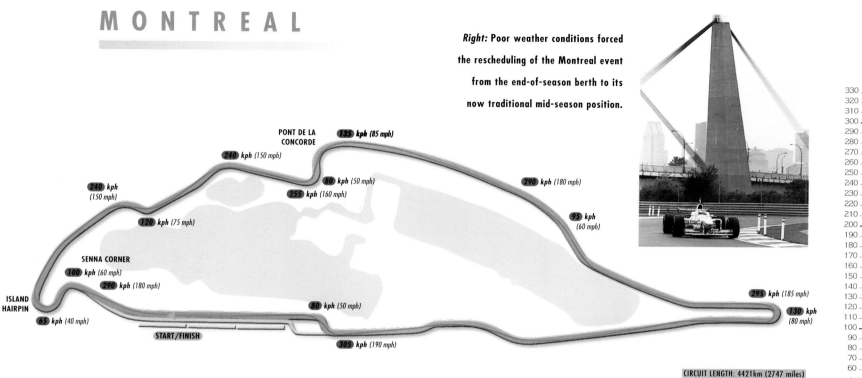

PONT DE LA
CONCORDE

**135** *kph (85 mph)*

**240** *kph (150 mph)*

**240** *kph*
*(150 mph)*

**290** *kph (180 mph)*

**80** *kph (50 mph)*

**255** *kph (160 mph)*

**120** *kph (75 mph)*

**95** *kph*
*(60 mph)*

SENNA CORNER

**100** *kph (60 mph)*

**290** *kph (180 mph)*

**295** *kph (185 mph)*

ISLAND
HAIRPIN

**80** *kph (50 mph)*

**130** *kph*
*(80 mph)*

**65** *kph (40 mph)*

START/FINISH

**305** *kph (190 mph)*

**CIRCUIT LENGTH: 4421km (2747 miles)**

hosted two world championship races, in 1968 (won by Denny Hulme in the McLaren-Ford) and 1970 (won by Jacky Ickx in a Ferrari). With the demise of Mont Tremblant, Mosport Park earned itself a permanent place on the calendar for the next seven years. No race was held in Canada in 1975.

**MONTREAL:** The focus of Canadian racing moved east to Montreal in 1978 and the 4.5km (2.8-mile) Ile de Notre Dame circuit built on a man-made island in the St Lawrence seaway. It is a tight, narrow track designed by Roger Peart and laid out among lakes and the parkland pavilions used for the World Expo '67 exhibition that run alongside the Olympic Rowing Strip used for the 1976 Olympics. One of the views most associated with Formula One in Canada is that of the pavilion, looking for all the world like a giant golf ball, as the backdrop to the cars rounding the hairpin.

There could not have been a more appropriate opening race, with Gilles Villeneuve driving the Ferrari in his first season in Formula One. He won, sending the crowds into raptures with his maiden victory.

There were several cosmetic changes for the 1979 race that, although won by Alan Jones in a Williams-Ford, will be remembered for Niki Lauda walking out of Formula One halfway through the race weekend.

Jones was triumphant again the following year. He actually finished second out on the course, but Didier Pironi, who took the chequered flag, was racing under a one-minute penalty for jumping the start. The race was also significant for the participation of 19-year-old Mike Thackwell who became the youngest man to race in a Formula One Grand Prix, although he made it no further than the first corner.

In 1981 Jacques Laffite scored his final Grand Prix victory in appalling weather with Villeneuve back in third place. Maybe because of inclement late-season weather in Canada the race was switched to its now traditional June slot for 1982.

**Above:** An unusual cross between street circuit and permanent road track, the Montreal racetrack is laid out on the Ile de Notre Dame, a man-made island in the St Lawrence seaway.

By the time the Formula One circus gathered in Montreal for the 1982 race, Gilles Villeneuve had lost his life at Zolder and, along with him, some of the glamour was missing.

So soon after the tragedy at Zolder, the last thing Formula One needed was another disaster – but that is exactly what happened. In pole position was Didier Pironi, but on the green light his Ferrari stalled and Riccardo Paletti, the 24-year-old Italian, ploughed into the back of him. Pironi, unhurt, leapt from his car to help the injured Paletti, but was held back when the cars burst into flames. The fire was soon put out and Paletti, racing in only his second Grand Prix, was taken to hospital but died soon afterwards. Victory on that sad afternoon went to Nelson Piquet in the Brabham-BMW.

Piquet scored his second Canadian triumph in 1984, again at the wheel of the Brabham-BMW. Seven years later he tied up his hat-trick of victories in the Benetton-Ford. The third win was remarkable: entering the last lap, Piquet was more than 30 seconds behind Nigel Mansell in the Williams-Renault. But as the Englishman triumphantly waved to the crowd acknowledging his victory, his car crawled to a dead halt allowing an astonished but delighted Piquet to race through and take the chequered flag.

Another three-time winner who can count Montreal among his most profitable circuits is Michael Schumacher, winner in 1994 for Benetton-Ford, and back-to-back in 1997 and 1998 aboard a Ferrari.

In 1987, a dispute between rival brewers and sponsors, Labatt's and Molson, caused the cancellation of the Grand Prix. Once the altercation had been settled the race returned for 1988, with a new pit complex.

That race was won by Ayrton Senna in a McLaren Honda on the way to his first world championship. He also came home in front two years later for his second Canadian Grand Prix win.

Prior to the 1991 race, a new corner was added before the pits and, in reaction to the fatalities at Imola in 1994, the circuit was slowed with a chicane along the straight leading back to the pits.

Perhaps Montreal's most emotional occasion in recent years was the afternoon of the memorable 1995 race, when Jean Alesi, driving the No 27 Ferrari made famous by local hero Gilles Villeneuve, scored his first, and to date only, Grand Prix victory.

*Below:* **The Benetton of Alexander Wurz is sent into a roll after a first corner collision in the 1999 Canadian Grand Prix. The accident also ended the race for Jean Alesi (Sauber) and Jarno Trulli (Prost).**

# INDIANAPOLIS

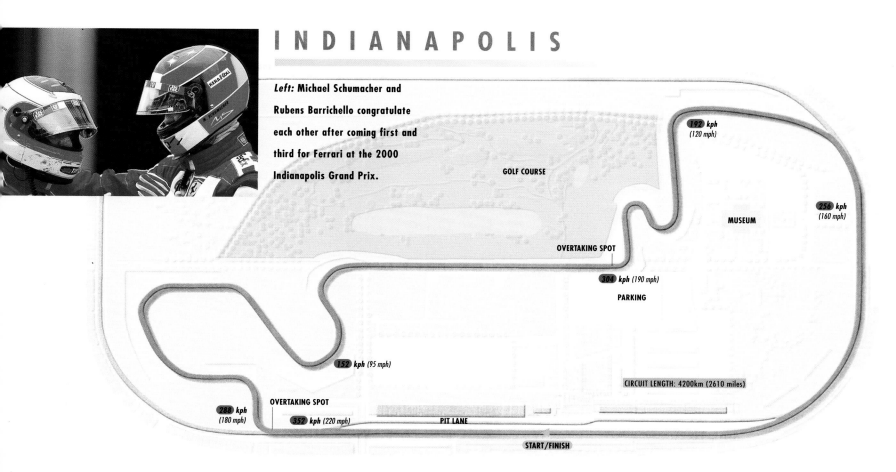

*Left:* Michael Schumacher and
Rubens Barrichello congratulate
each other after coming first and
third for Ferrari at the 2000
Indianapolis Grand Prix.

GOLF COURSE

**192** *kph* *(120 mph)*

**256** *kph* *(160 mph)*

MUSEUM

OVERTAKING SPOT

**304** *kph (190 mph)*

PARKING

**152** *kph (95 mph)*

CIRCUIT LENGTH: 4200km (2610 miles)

OVERTAKING SPOT

**288** *kph* *(180 mph)*

**352** *kph (220 mph)*

PIT LANE

START/FINISH

# USA

There are many famous race tracks in the United States. Indianapolis and Daytona are known the world over, but until now they have restricted their activities to Indycar and NASCAR races, respectively. Since the demise of the most famous of American Grand Prix venues, Watkins Glen, in 1980, the American Grand Prix has had a tendency to wander. Since the halcyon days of the late 1970s and early 1980s, eight years went by in the 1990s without a single Grand Prix.

Thanks to an agreement between Tony George, the Indianapolis track owner, and Bernie Ecclestone, ringmaster of Formula One, that situation has been remedied. Formula One is back in the USA, at one of the world's best-known racetracks, the Indianapolis Motor Speedway. A purpose-built track on the infield at Indianapolis, which makes use of one of the outer track's famous turns, was constructed for the USA Grand Prix of 2000, won by Michael Schumacher.

**SEBRING:** The first Grand Prix to be held in the United States was run at Sebring in Florida in 1959. The Sebring circuit was conceived by Alex Ulmann and opened for racing in December 1950. It consisted of a series of concrete runways and tarmac roads that had comprised the World War II aerodrome, Hendrick Field. Before and after its sole Formula One event, it has been home to the famous Sebring 12-hour sports car race.

The 1959 Grand Prix was scene of Bruce McLaren's debut Formula

*Above:* **The Formula One racetrack at Indianapolis, constructed within the oval Indianapolis Motor Speedway track.**
*Right:* **An aerial view of the world famous Indianapolis Motor Speedway. The inaugural Grand Prix in 2000 attracted a record 222,000 spectators.**

One victory, driving a Cooper Climax. In the same race, Jack Brabham secured the world championship when he pushed his car over the finish line.

RIVERSIDE: The following year, Formula One moved across America to California and the Riverside track. Purpose-built in 1957, this 5.3km (3.29-mile) circuit lay 97km (60 miles) east of Los Angeles and its main straight doubled as a drag strip. The only Grand Prix to be held there in 1960 was won by Stirling Moss in a Lotus Climax. Located deep in the hilly desert country, which made corner marking difficult, Riverside fell into disrepair and was closed in 1988.

WATKINS GLEN: The first true home of the United States Grand Prix was Watkins Glen, which hosted the first of its 20 races in 1961. The track, which nestles among the hills above Lake Seneca in the Finger Lakes region of upstate New York, was conceived by Cameron Argetsinger in 1947. The original 10.5km (6.5 mile) road course was dismantled after a series of accidents, and in 1953 a purpose-built 3.5km (2.3-mile) track, designed by Bill Miliken, was opened. It hosted its first Grand Prix in 1961, a race won by Innes Ireland in a Lotus.

Over the next seven years British drivers dominated the race, with Jim Clark and Graham Hill winning three times, as well as a sole victory for Jackie Stewart. This streak of British luck was brought to

an end in 1969 by Lotus' Jochen Rindt, but the race was marred by the horrifying accident that left Rindt's team-mate, Graham Hill, seriously injured after being thrown from his car after a puncture.

The race of 1970, won by Emerson Fittipaldi, was the last on the original circuit. During the summer of 1970 the track went though an extensive redevelopment programme, which included a new 1.8km (1.1-mile) four-corner section. The facelift was no mere cosmetic operation; it turned an average track into a really demanding one.

The first race on the new track was won by François Cevert in his Tyrrell; two years later he lost his life in the qualifying rounds at the venue. His team-mate, Jackie Stewart, had planned to retire at the end of what would have been his 100th Grand Prix start, but as a result of Cevert's tragic death Tyrrell withdrew their cars, and Stewart's

*Below:* **Alain Prost in the McLaren MP4/5 leads around the much maligned Phoenix street circuit in 1989. When Ayrton Senna retired with electrical problems after 44 laps, victory went to Prost and the McLaren team.**

career was brought to an end under a cloud of tragedy.

A chicane was added after the 1973 tragedy, but the next year yet another driver, Helmut Koinigg, was killed at Watkins Glen. Safety concerns aside, the venue was also not ideal for the exacting demands of sponsors and the notoriously squalid bog surrounding it hardly befitted the sport's glamour image. Alan Jones won the last Formula One race at the Glen, in 1980.

**LONG BEACH:** In 1976 Long Beach debuted in Formula One at the 'US West Grand Prix'. An industrial seaport south of Los Angeles, Long Beach was anxious to enhance its appeal as its only attractions had been the Queen Mary berthed in its harbour and the presence of Howard Hughes' enormous seaplane, Spruce Goose. Chris Pook, an Englishman, convinced the city fathers that a Grand Prix would be good for the image and, after a trial run with a Formula 5000 race in 1975, Formula One roared onto the streets of Long Beach.

The first year's event was a disappointment, but after an exciting 1977 race won by an American, Mario Andretti, the race became

extremely popular. In 1980 Long Beach was the scene of Nelson Piquet's first Grand Prix win, but unfortunately also the career-ending accident that left Clay Regazzoni confined to a wheelchair.

The huge cost of running world-class races led to the end of the career of Long Beach as a Formula One venue after the 1983 race. Following the demise of Watkins Glen, the United States Grand Prix began a cross country trek through one dreary street venue after another, without locating a suitable track or an audience who wanted to watch Formula One races.

**LAS VEGAS:** Las Vegas was top of the league. The track there, built within the Caesar's Palace Hotel car park, was temporary, made out of interlocking concrete barriers. The circuit ran anti-clockwise, doubling back on itself within tight confines. Despite its lack of appeal, the two races held in Las Vegas were both title deciders. In 1981 Piquet came in fifth to win the title by just one point from Carlos Reutemann, and in 1982 Rosberg made fifth place to claim the title (and a kiss from Diana Ross), with Didier Pironi just five points adrift.

**DETROIT:** Detroit was the next venue to try to win the hearts and minds of the Formula One faithful. A street circuit in downtown Motown was a good marketing idea, but the right-angled nature of the circuit did not allow Formula One cars to demonstrate the full range of their abilities. In spite of its tunnel and its waterside location, this was no Monaco. Senna thrived there, winning three races in a row from 1986, the first two in the Lotus and the third in a McLaren. Others, among them Prost and Piquet, detested the track. When the race left for Phoenix in 1988, it was used as an Indycar venue before that moved to its current location at Belle Isle.

During Detroit's reign, a street track at Dallas made a brief appearance on the Formula One scene. The 4km (2.4-mile) track was located in the Fair Park area of the city. A typically angular street circuit, it

**Top right: Alan Jones in action at the 1981 US West Grand Prix at Long Beach. Jones won the race in the Williams FW07C ahead of team-mate Carlos Reutemann, with Nelson Piquet third in the Brabham BT49C.**

was used only once, in 1984. The race was less than successful – the track surface broke up badly, causing all sorts of problems for the drivers, before Rosberg came home in front, in the Williams.

**PHOENIX:** Phoenix was the next target. Yet another tight street circuit laid out between concrete barriers, it was not likely to succeed and didn't. Phoenix never proved popular with drivers and spectators and, even after an attempt to rearrange the circuit with fewer right-hand corners for the 1991 race, Formula One organizers abandoned it as a bad idea. The three races held here were dominated by the McLaren team with Prost winning the inaugural race in 1989 and Senna winning the other two.

The departure from Phoenix marked the start of the United States' eight-year gap on the Formula One calendar, a situation that Bernie Ecclestone was at pains to redress. Several venues attempted to lure Formula One back to America, including Brandy Station, near Washington, and Las Vegas (again), before a deal was struck for a dramatic Grand Prix resurrection at Indianapolis for the 2000 season.

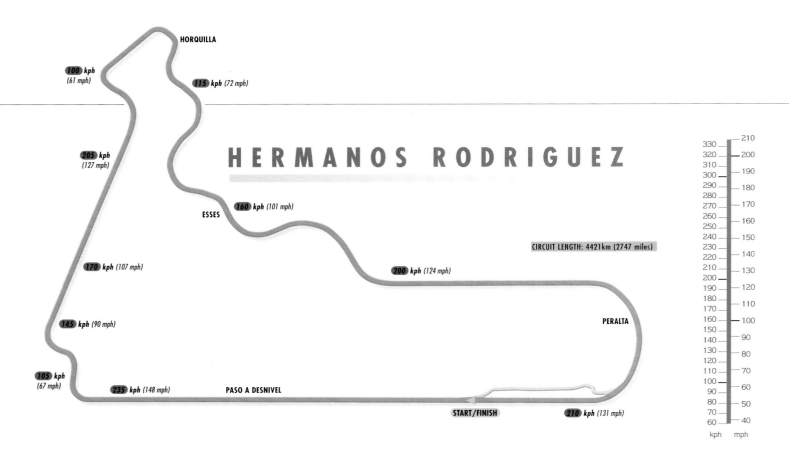

HORQUILLA

100 kph (61 mph)

115 kph (72 mph)

# HERMANOS RODRIGUEZ

205 kph (127 mph)

160 kph (101 mph)

ESSES

CIRCUIT LENGTH: 4421km (2747 miles)

170 kph (107 mph)

200 kph (124 mph)

145 kph (90 mph)

PERALTA

105 kph (67 mph)

235 kph (148 mph)

PASO A DESNIVEL

START/FINISH

210 kph (131 mph)

| kph | mph |
|---|---|
| 330 | 210 |
| 320 | 200 |
| 310 | 190 |
| 300 | |
| 290 | 180 |
| 280 | |
| 270 | 170 |
| 260 | 160 |
| 250 | |
| 240 | 150 |
| 230 | |
| 220 | 140 |
| 210 | 130 |
| 200 | |
| 190 | 120 |
| 180 | 110 |
| 170 | |
| 160 | 100 |
| 150 | |
| 140 | 90 |
| 130 | 80 |
| 120 | |
| 110 | 70 |
| 100 | |
| 90 | 60 |
| 80 | 50 |
| 70 | |
| 60 | 40 |

# MEXICO

Mexico City is one of the world's most overcrowded cities, a smog-filled metropolis that was hardly the ideal venue for the sport of the rich and famous. That, and the sometimes unruly nature of the spectators, meant that Mexico was always existing on borrowed time as a Grand Prix location. As if those negative aspects were not enough, there was also the constant fear of crippling stomach bugs – a potential threat to the paddock at every race.

'In Mexico you had to be careful about how you lived,' John Surtees said of the city. 'You watched what you ate and drank, you didn't touch the water and that was always one of my concerns at the Mexican Grand Prix.'

Another problem was altitude. The track lies at 2286m (7500ft) above sea level which causes a significant loss of engine power, as

*Above:* **The Hermanos Rodriguez racetrack in Mexico City is known for its fast final corner, which leads into a long pit straight.**
*Right:* **Nigel Mansell takes the chequered flag at the end of the 1987 Mexican Grand Prix. Formula One left Mexico for good five years later.**

Graham Hill explained: 'There just isn't enough air to get sucked into the engine. Roughly, you end up with the engine 25 per cent down on power. This affects every car the same way, or is supposed to, but we normally found that with the multi-cylinder cars, the 12-cylinders, for instance, are slightly better off than the 8-cylinder cars.'

**HERMANOS RODRIGUEZ:** The 4.98km (3.1-mile) Magdalena Mixhuca circuit is situated in a municipal sports park, built on a dried-up lake bed. In its early days there were always crowd problems; this factor, together with its very bumpy surface, meant that its career as a racetrack was brief.

In the early 1960s, motor racing in Mexico focused on two talented brothers, Pedro and Ricardo Rodriguez. When Mexico City first played host to a world championship race, what began as a carnival, ended in tragedy when the erratic Ricardo, 20, was killed during the qualifying laps. Jim Clark won that race in his Lotus 25 Climax.

The end-of-season berth the race occupied meant that the races were usually fraught with tension. In fact, over the next seven years, until Mexico lost the Grand Prix in 1970, no less than three world championships were decided in the Mexican capital.

The first was in 1964 when three drivers (Graham Hill in a BRM on 39 points, John Surtees in a Ferrari with 34, and Lotus driver Clark with 30), all had a chance to take the title at the Mexican Grand Prix. The calculations were more complicated than a first glance would reveal, because these were the days in which only one's best six results counted towards the championship. Hill already had six finishes to his name and so would be forced to drop his worst points-scoring finish (the three points he had won in Holland), while Surtees and Clark had only five and four points-scoring finishes respectively.

Clark started the race on the front row, with Surtees on the row behind and Hill on row three. Clark, the reigning world champion, shot into the lead, leaving his two protagonists trailing in 10th (Hill) and 13th (Surtees) place by the end of the first lap. Hill's race effectively came to an end on lap 30 when Bandini, in the second Ferrari, sent him crashing into the guardrail at the hairpin. Hill kept going, but in his damaged BRM he could only hope that neither of his rivals made it to the finish. In front Clark reigned supreme, apparently on his way to retaining the championship. However, with two laps remaining, the Lotus slowed with a broken oil pipe. Surtees roared past and up to third spot as they started the final lap. All that now stood between Surtees and the world championship was Bandini, his team-mate. Stories differ as to whether Bandini slowed to let the Englishman past or whether a final, frantic effort secured a pass, but the net result was that Surtees crossed the line in second place, behind Dan Gurney. On an afternoon of high drama, he had won his only world championship.

Richie Ginther scored Honda's first Grand Prix win in 1965, John Surtees winning in 1966. Mexico's next title decider was in 1967, Denny Hulme trailing his team-mate, and title challenger, Jack Brabham, over the line in third place to claim the championship.

The following year the title was again up for grabs. Graham Hill came into the race three points clear of his closest rival, Matra driver Jackie Stewart. There was none of the drama of four years earlier, when Hill won the race 40 seconds clear of Bruce McLaren. Denny Hulme in a McLaren and Jacky Ickx in Ferrari rounded off Mexico's first stint as a world championship venue.

Formula One returned 16 years later to the renamed (in memory of the Rodriguez brothers) Circuito Hermanos Ricardo y Pedro Rodriguez. It had also enjoyed a facelift with a revised 4.4km (2.73-mile) layout. This time around the track survived for seven years, Nigel Mansell winning the final Formula One race at the circuit in 1992.

# INTERLAGOS

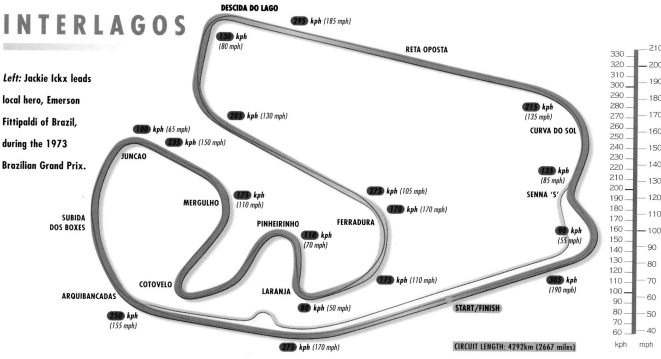

*Left: Jackie Ickx leads local hero, Emerson Fittipaldi of Brazil, during the 1973 Brazilian Grand Prix.*

DESCIDA DO LAGO
**295** kph *(185 mph)*
**130** kph *(80 mph)*
RETA OPOSTA
**205** kph *(130 mph)*
**215** kph *(135 mph)*
CURVA DO SOL
**100** kph *(65 mph)*
**235** kph *(150 mph)*
JUNCAO
**135** kph *(85 mph)*
SENNA 'S'
**275** kph *(105 mph)*
**175** kph *(110 mph)*
MERGULHO
**170** kph *(170 mph)*
**90** kph *(55 mph)*
SUBIDA DOS BOXES
PINHEIRINHO
FERRADURA
**110** kph *(70 mph)*
COTOVELO
**175** kph *(110 mph)*
**305** kph *(190 mph)*
ARQUIBANCADAS
LARANJA
**250** kph *(155 mph)*
**80** kph *(50 mph)*
START/FINISH
**275** kph *(170 mph)*
CIRCUIT LENGTH: 4292km (2667 miles)

kph | mph
330 — 210
320 — 200
310
300 — 190
290 — 180
280
270 — 170
260 — 160
250
240 — 150
230
220 — 140
210 — 130
200
190 — 120
180 — 110
170
160 — 100
150
140 — 90
130
120 — 80
110 — 70
100
90 — 60
80 — 50
70
60 — 40

# BRAZIL

The Brazilian Grand Prix has had two spiritual homes over the years, one in each of its two major cities: the Interlagos track in São Paulo and Jacarepagua in Rio de Janeiro. In modern terms, it comes as a surprise that the Formula One world championship had been in action 23 years before it paid its first visit to Brazil, prompted by the success of Brazilian drivers, principally Emerson Fittipaldi.

**INTERLAGOS AND JACAREPAGUA:** The Interlagos circuit was built in a natural bowl that has gradually been absorbed by the polluted and overcrowded city. The original 8km (4.95-mile) track twisted between two lakes, and had hosted several noteworthy non-championship races in 1971 and 1972, the latter won by Carlos Reutemann.

When the world championship race first arrived in Brazil the following year, it was reigning world champion, Fittipaldi, who sent the crowd into raptures when he brought his JPS Lotus 72D home in front of the man destined to succeed him, Jackie Stewart, in the Tyrrell 005. He repeated the feat the following year, this time aboard

a McLaren M23, the early-season victory setting him on his way to a second world championship.

Carlos Pace completed the hat-trick of wins by Brazilians in 1975, bringing the Brabham BT44B home in front of the McLarens of Fittipaldi and Jochen Mass. His only Formula One victory, Pace lost his life two years later in an aeroplane crash. Two Ferrari victories, Niki Lauda in the Ferrari 312T in 1976 and Carlos Reutemann in the 312T2, rounded off Interlagos' first stint as a Formula One venue.

Time for Brazil's second track to step into the limelight. Also known as the Autodromo International de Rio, Jacarepagua was built in the late 1970s on reclaimed marshland about 1.6km (1 mile) from the sea, hidden from the beauty and vibrancy that is the hallmark of the Brazilian city of Rio de Janeiro. Unfortunately, the track is typical of many modern facilities: flat, uniform, beset with constant radius corners and dominated by an extremely long main straight.

*Above: The Interlagos track in São Paulo was reshaped in 1990 and today hosts the Brazilian Grand Prix, raced anti-clockwise around the circuit.*
*Right: Hot air balloons float above the Jacarepagua track during the 1987 Grand Prix, won by Alain Prost in the McLaren, as Brazilian fans pack the stands to support local heroes Nelson Piquet and Ayrton Senna.*

Formula One first came to Rio in 1978 and, to the disappointment of the excitable crowds, Argentinian Carlos Reutemann took victory ahead of local idol Emerson Fittipaldi, driving his family's team car, the F5A.

After the brief experiment with Jacarepagua, the teams were back at Interlagos for two races in 1979 and 1980. Jacques Laffite won in 1979, following up his season-opening win at Buenos Aires with the second leg of the South American double. Another Frenchman, René Arnoux, took the honours in a Renault RE20 turbo in 1980.

When the Grand Prix returned to Jacarepagua after its sojourn at Interlagos, Fittipaldi was no longer racing and local fans had a new idol in Nelson Piquet. He duly placed his Brabham BT49C in pole

position ahead of his old enemy, Reutemann. On race day it rained and, in a brave move, Piquet elected to start the race on dry tyres, hoping for a change in weather. Unfortunately for Piquet and his passionate fans, the weather did not improve. Worse for the locals, with Piquet out of the way the scene was set for Reutemann to lead from start to finish.

The following year the weather was a complete contrast. The sun was so hot that Riccardo Patrese passed out from heat exhaustion and spun out after just 29 laps. At the front of the field, the two normally aspirated cars, the Brabham BT49D of Piquet and the Williams FW07C of Keke Rosberg, were battling against the turbo-charged

Renault RE30B of Alain Prost. By the fall of the chequered flag Piquet had squeezed himself in front and led Rosberg home, sending the crowd into ecstasy. Two months later both Piquet and Rosberg were disqualified for underweight cars, but that mattered little to the fans packing the grandstand on this day.

Piquet repeated the feat the following year, again ahead of Rosberg, setting up a six-year sequence in which he and Alain Prost would dominate this race. Piquet won again in 1986, this time in a Williams FW11 ahead of the new Brazilian superstar Ayrton Senna in the Lotus 98T, and Prost cleaned up in 1984, 1985, 1987 and 1988, each time in a McLaren. Piquet's success prompted the renaming of the track in his honour, in 1988. In what was to be Jacarepagua's final Grand Prix, Nigel Mansell scored a dramatic and unexpected victory in 1989 in his Ferrari debut.

The focus of racing in Brazil returned to a reshaped Interlagos in 1990 and has remained there ever since. The track, now swallowed up by the sprawling city, had been remodelled to 4.3km (2.67 miles), eliminating much of the original layout, but preserving the sweeping uphill start-finish straight.

Until the death of Ayrton Senna in 1994, the race was always a noisy, passionate affair, but since then it has lost its charm and intensity. This was only fully rekindled in the 2000 season when Brazilian Rubens Barrichello raced alongside Michael Schumacher for Ferrari.

In fact, Schumacher has become the most successful modern driver at Interlagos with his victories in 1994 and 1995 in the Benetton and aboard the Ferrari for the 2000 race. Two McLaren men, Senna in 1991 and 1993 and Hakkinen in 1998 and 1999, have claimed victories in a race that is particularly demanding on drivers because of the unusual anti-clockwise direction of the track.

*Left:* **Formula One returned to São Paulo, Ayrton Senna's home town, in 1990 after a 10-year absence – up until his death in 1994 the race was a vibrant, colourful and noisy affair.**
*Right:* **Ferrari driver Jean Alesi in action on Formula One's return to Argentina in 1995.**

# AUTODROMO OSCAR GALVEZ, BUENOS AIRES

255 kph (160 mph)
275 kph (170 mph)
275 kph (170 mph)
145 kph (90 mph)
110 kph (70 mph)
CAJON
150 kph (95 mph)
135 kph (85 mph)
75 kph (45 mph)
240 kph (150 mph)
SENNA 'S'
235 kph (150 mph)
CURVA DE LA CONFITERIA
90 kph (55 mph)
290 kph (180 mph)
START/FINISH
215 kph (135 mph)
240 kph (150 mph)
70 kph (45 mph)
CIRCUIT LENGTH: 4259km (2647 miles)

# ARGENTINA

For a country that has produced such famous racers as Juan Manuel Fangio, José Froilan Gonzáles and Carlos Reutemann, Argentina has had a sketchy Grand Prix history. It has only ever possessed one track capable of hosting a Formula One event, although that has appeared in various guises.

The construction of Argentina's racing heritage was overseen by President Juan Domingo Peron. The Autodromo Almirante (Admiral) Brown, or to give it its original name, El Autodromo 17 de Octobre (the date of Peron's accession), was built on swampland on the outskirts of Buenos Aires. When it opened in March 1952 it featured 12 configurations. The original Grand Prix configuration was a 4km (2.48-mile) clockwise layout.

**AUTODROMO OSCAR GALVEZ:** The Autodromo hosted its first Formula One championship race in 1953. Local hero Fangio was favourite but he was forced to retire and victory went to Alberto Ascari. The following year, Fangio won in a Maserati to the delight of

Argentinian racing legend in the making, Carlos Reutemann, made his debut in a hired McLaren.

Reutemann was back in 1972, in the Brabham BT137, to trail home in seventh place, two laps behind the winner, Jackie Stewart, driving a Tyrrell. Although Reutemann ran the home race on nine occasions, unlike Fangio he was destined never to win there. At least there was a South American victor in 1973, when Brazilian Emerson Fittipaldi won in the Lotus.

The track marked another milestone in 1974 when Denny Hulme won the season-opening race in the Mclaren MP23, his eighth and final Grand Prix victory in what was to prove to be his last season in Formula One racing.

the legions of adoring fans who watched him compete in his home Grand Prix. The fans went wild when he repeated the feat the following year, this time driving a Mercedes. The race became a one-man show, with Fangio claiming top honours in 1956 in the Ferrari and again in 1957 with Maserati.

In what was to be his final Argentinian Grand Prix, Fangio took pole position in his Maserati. He set the fastest lap, but failed to get his fifth victory in a row due to mechanical problems. The prize went to his rival, Stirling Moss, in a Cooper Climax. This was a landmark win for the British driver, as it was the first Formula One triumph for a rear-engined car. Formula One then left Buenos Aires for 13 years.

In 1972 a 'different' championship returned to a much-altered track. The revamped circuit, which had been swallowed up by the burgeoning city, had returned to international prominence the year before, hosting several non-championship Formula One races. In a Buenos Aires 1000, Ignazio Giunti, the Italian Ferrari driver, lost his life running into Jean-Pierre Beltoise's Matra that had flouted the rules by being pushed on the track. A few weeks later, in another non-championship race, Chris Amon won in a Matra while the new

*Above:* **Michael Schumacher leading the 1995 Argentinian Grand Prix, driving for the Benetton team.**
*Right:* **The start of the 1995 Argentinian Grand Prix at the Autodromo Oscar Galvez, which featured a shorter configuration of the former track, was won in style by Damon Hill.**

Argentina did not host a race in the 1976 Grand Prix season; however, the following year saw the sensational debut of the Wolf team. Walter Wolf, a Canadian oil plant manufacturer, had purchased the Hesketh team's equipment and cars, along with talented designer, Harvey Postlethwaite. They had a new car, the WR1, and a brand new driver in future world champion Jody Scheckter, whom they had persuaded to leave Tyrrell to take his chances with the fledgling outfit. Scheckter won the Argentinian Grand Prix, the opening round of the season, ahead of Carlos Pace in the Brabham BT45 and Reutemann's Ferrari 312T2.

This was to prove a false dawn for Wolf. Although they won two more races that year, they survived for only three years. Racing 47 times, they notched up only three victories.

Two years later, Buenos Aires was the scene of another twist with French Formula One fortunes revived after the victory of Jacques Laffite in the ground effects JS11 Ligier, the marque's second victory.

The year 1980 was a low point for motorsport in Argentina after the track broke up during the race. Piquet won the following year in the Brabham, on the way to his first championship.

Grand Prix returned for a four-year stint in 1995. The new tight, narrow and twisty track, renamed the Autodromo Oscar Galvez, proved unpopular and unsuited to modern Formula One machines. The final race there, in 1998, was won by Michael Schumacher in a Ferrari.

# INDEX

*Previous pages:* The heat was on for Michael Schumacher in the final Grand Prix of the 2000 season, held at Sepang in Malaysia. With the World Championship already secured, Schumacher claimed another great win in the humid heat of Malaysia to secure the Constructors' title for Ferrari.

# CREDITS AND ACKNOWLEDGEMENTS

**KEY TO PHOTOGRAPHERS** (Copyright © rests with the following photographers and/or their agents): TL/AS=Touchline/Allsport (MC=Michael Cooper); BC=Bernard Cahier; PHC=Paul-Henri Cahier; DD=Derek Dallas; JFW=Jutta Fausel-Ward; Fer=Ferrari/Maranello; GPL=The GP Library; ICN=!CN; LAT=LAT (ST=Steven Tee); LL=Ludvigsen Library (MIG=Max le Grand); SP=Sporting Pictures (MH=M Hewett; PV=P Vincent); MV=Mark Venables. **KEY TO LOCATIONS:** t=top; tl=top left; tc=top centre; tr=top right; c=centre; bl=bottom left; bc=bottom centre; br=bottom right; l=left; r=right; b=bottom; i=inset; bgi=background image. (No abbreviation is given for pages with a single image.)

| | | | | | | | | | | | |
|---|---|---|---|---|---|---|---|---|---|---|---|
| **Endpapers** | | LAT | | br | LAT | **72:** | t | TL/AS/MC | **112:** | t | LdL/MIG |
| **1:** | | SP | **39:** | | LAT | | b | SP | | b | LAT |
| **2:** | | LAT | **40:** | | LdL/MIG | **73:** | | MV | **113:** | | LAT |
| **4:** | | PHC | **41:** | t | JFW | **74:** | t | LdL/MIG | **114:** | | SP |
| **6:** | | JFW | | b | GPL | | b | SP | **115:** | | GPL |
| **8:** | | ICN | **42:** | | LAT | **75:** | t | SP | **117:** | | GPL |
| **10–11:** | | PHC | **43:** | t | BC | | b | TL/AS/MC | **119:** | | GPL |
| **12:** | | SP | | i | MV | **76:** | | PHC | **120:** | | MV |
| **14:** | tl | GPL | **45:** | | LAT | **77:** | l | ICN | **121:** | | LAT |
| | tc | SP | | i | BC | | r | PHC | **122–23:** | | GPL |
| | tr | GPL | **46:** | t | SP | **78:** | t | JFW | **124:** | | LAT |
| | bl | BC | | b | LdL/MIG | | b | GPL | **126:** | t | LAT |
| **15:** | tl | GPL | **47:** | | JFW | **79:** | tl | MV | | b | SP |
| | tc | GPL | **48:** | tl | LAT | | tr | JFW | **127:** | | GPL |
| | tr | BC | | tr | SP | | b | SP | **128:** | b | MV |
| **16:** | | LAT | | b | SP | **80:** | | MV | | i | ICN |
| **17:** | tl | BC | **49:** | tl | JFW | **81:** | t | LAT/ST | **129:** | | SP |
| | bl | SP | | tr | SP | | b | SP | **130:** | | ICN |
| | tr | JFW | **50:** | | JFW | **82:** | t | SP | **131:** | tl | SP |
| | br | JFW | **51:** | t | JFW | | b | LdL/MIG | | tc | SP |
| **18:** | | LAT | | b | PHC | **83:** | | GPL | | tr | SP |
| **19:** | tl | SP | **52:** | | GPL | **84–85:** | | PHC | | b | SP |
| | tr | PHC | **53:** | t | SP | **86:** | | SP | **132:** | | MV |
| **20–21:** | | SP | | b | SP | **88:** | | TL/AS/MC | **133:** | | SP |
| **22:** | | JFW | **54:** | | MV | **89:** | | LAT | **134:** | t | MV |
| **24:** | tl | LAT | **55:** | l | MV | **90:** | | PHC | | b | LAT |
| | tc | LAT | | r | MV | **91:** | | MV | **135:** | | PHC |
| | tr | BC | **56:** | t | MV | **92:** | | MV | **136–37:** | | PHC |
| **25:** | tl | JFW | | bl | SP | **94:** | | LAT | **138:** | | SP |
| | tc | LAT | | br | PHC | **95:** | | MV | **140:** | | MV |
| | tr | ICN | **57:** | | GPL | **96:** | | MV | **141:** | | GPL |
| **26:** | | JFW | **58:** | t | SP | **97:** | | LAT | **142:** | tl | PHC |
| **27:** | tl | JFW | | b | PHC | **98:** | t | LAT | **143:** | | PHC |
| | bl | MV | **59:** | | PHC | | b | MV | **144:** | | GPL |
| **28:** | | MV | **60:** | | MV | **99:** | | GPL | **145:** | | JFW |
| **29:** | tr | MV | **61:** | | PHC | **101:** | | GPL | **146–47:** | | JFW |
| | br | MV | **62:** | | SP | **102:** | | PHC | **148:** | | LAT |
| **30–31:** | b | LAT | **63:** | | TL/AS | **103:** | | MV | **149:** | | SP |
| | tl | MV | **64:** | | SP | **105:** | | MV | **150:** | | GPL |
| | tr | MV | **65:** | | PHC | **106:** | | DD | **151:** | | GPL |
| **32–33:** | | GPL | **66:** | t | PHC | | bgi | SP | **152:** | tl | GPL |
| **34:** | | BC | | b | PHC | **107:** | | DD | **152–153:** | b | MV |
| **36:** | t | BC | **67:** | | PHC | **108:** | | ICN | **154–155:** | | PHC |
| | b | GPL | **68:** | | PHC | **109:** | | MV | **156:** | | LL |
| **37:** | | LAT | **69:** | | GPL | **110:** | | LAT | **158:** | | LL |
| **38:** | tl | LAT | **70:** | | LAT | **111:** | | SP | **160:** | | GPL |

**PUBLISHERS' ACKNOWLEDGEMENTS:** The publishers are grateful for the cooperation received from many sources. In particular, the sterling efforts of the consultant editors and fact checkers and the helpful image libraries who supplied picture material. A special word of thanks to Luigi Viglietti of Viglietti Motors, official Ferrari dealer in Cape Town, South Africa, for his enthusiasm and generous supply of reference material.